Anonymous

A Guide to the City of Chicago

Its public Buildings, Places of Amusement, etc.

Anonymous

A Guide to the City of Chicago
Its public Buildings, Places of Amusement, etc.

ISBN/EAN: 9783337130589

Printed in Europe, USA, Canada, Australia, Japan

Cover: Foto ©ninafisch / pixelio.de

More available books at **www.hansebooks.com**

SEYMOUR, CARTER & CO.

DEALERS IN

HOSIERY,
GLOVES,
WHITE GOODS,
LINENS,

SHIRTS AND DRAWERS, HOOP SKIRTS,

CORSETS, NOTIONS, &C.,

No. 22 LAKE ST.,

CHICAGO.

THOMAS H. SEYMOUR, }
THOMAS B. CARTER, }

{ JAMES TWAMLEY,
{ THOMAS H. DOANE.

BELDING BROTHERS & CO.,
MANUFACTURERS & JOBBERS OF
SEWING SILKS,
MACHINE TWIST, &c.,
No. 54 Lake Street,   *CHICAGO.*

323 Broadway, New York; 95 & 97 Pearl St., Cincinnati.
MILLS, Willimantic, Conn.

M. M. BELDING,   Orders will meet with prompt   A. N. BELDING;
H. H. BELDING,   attention.   W. A. STANTON.

SWEDISH MOVEMENT CURE,
FOR THE TREATMENT OF CHRONIC DISEASES, LOCAL AND GENERAL WEAKNESS, AND SPINAL DEFORMITIES.

The *Movement Cure* is a *system* of *medical practice*, by which *remedial effects* are obtained by the *scientific* and *systematic* application of *motion.*

Prominent among the cases treated are *Spinal Curvatures, Distorted Shoulders, Weak Lungs. Paralysis,* Constipation, *Dyspepsia, Torpidity of Liver, Rheumatism, Imperfect Circulation,* all *Nervous Affections,* and *all Weaknesses of Women and Children.*

For *Spinal Curvatures,* it is the only *rational treatment.*

For *Nervous Diseases,* it is the most *effectual* remedy.

For *enlarging the Chest* and *strengthening weak Lungs,* it is the only means.

Children with *small, flabby Muscles, narrow Chests,* and *low vitality,* are *rapidly* and *permanently* improved.

Ladies in *delicate health* will find substantial relief in the *careful* and at length *thorough* exercises of the MOVEMENT CURE.

We have had great experience in our profession, having heretofore managed the largest and most successful institution of the kind in New England.

Our rooms are large and pleasant, and apparatus perfect and complete. Any further information cheerfully given upon application either personally or by letter.

Drs. J. G. & T. H. TRINE, Physicians and Proprietors,
Major Block, Cor. Madison and Lasalle Sts.,
CHICAGO, ILL.

Novelty Carriage Works

44 Adams Street, Chicago,

THOMAS H. BROWN, AGENT,

Keeps constantly on hand a fine assortment of

BUGGIES.

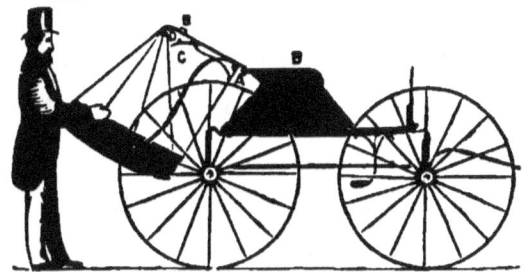

These works have received all the first Premiums for work exhibited at the Illinois State Fairs for the last three years.

Special attention given to the manufacture of

Sulkies, Skeleton Wagons, and Light Work of all descriptions.

All of the best and thoroughly seasoned timber, newest styles, and superior workmanship.

Grant's Shifting Buggy Top Rail,

(See Cut) by which the Top can be taken off and put on in one moment, and be as secure as if riveted to the seat. Shop Rights for the same can be had for the State of Illinois, at 44 Adams Street.

DR. J. PHILLIPS,

PRACTICAL OPTICIAN AND OCULIST,

168 S. Clark Street, Chicago.

Spectacles suited by Inspection of the Eye.

"There's no such word as fail." This saying is verified, and every person can call and see the proof, that DR. JOHN PHILLIPS will suit you with SPECTACLES by Inspection of the Eye. Over 1000 persons can testify to the truth of this statement in this city.

"We take pleasure in recommending DR. JOHN PHILLIPS as a superior Optician and a safe practical Oculist.
"President ABRAHAM LINCOLN.
"Governor RICHARD YATES."

AMERICAN TEA HOUSE.

HORACE MEECH,

WHOLESALE AND RETAIL DEALER IN

Tea, Coffee, Spices, Cream Tartar, Broma, Chocolate, Mustard, &c.

81 & 83 Monroe, and 171 Dearborn Sts.,

Cor. Monroe & Dearborn.   CHICAGO.   Opp. the Post-office.

"KNOWLEDGE IS POWER."

MACKENZIE'S 10,000 RECEIPTS,

In all the Useful and Domestic Arts; constituting a Complete and Practical Library, relating to Agriculture, Horticulture, Cements. Bleaching and Dyeing, Brewing, Cookery, Carving, Confectionery, Fish Culture, Farriery, Medicines, Oils, Paints and Varnishes, Metallurgy, Perfumery, Preserving, Tanning, Photography, Wines and Liquors, &c., &c., &c. Being an entirely New Edition, carefully revised and re-written by a Corps of Experts. Date of present issue, January 1, 1868, with Addition of Special Articles upon Bees, their Management; Farming Implements; the Rinderpest and Trichinæ.

It is unquestionably the BEST BOOK OF THE KIND EVER PUBLISHED. Every care has been taken in the compilation; the receipts have been critically examined by a scientific and practical corps of Editors and Authors.

Over forty persons have been employed upon this book; the list embraces some of the most distinguished scientific men of the country.

For Circulars containing a full description, address,

T. ELLWOOD ZELL & CO., Publishers,
17 & 19 S. *Sixth Street, Philadelphia.*

☞ Canvassers and Agents of character and ability wanted in the Cities, Counties, and Townships of the Union.

To be had of the Agents only.

BEAN, BROWNSON & CO.,
MANUFACTURERS OF
HOOP SKIRTS AND CORSETS,
58 MICHIGAN AVE., CHICAGO,
HAVE THE
LARGEST STOCK WEST OF NEW YORK CITY,
AND SELL THEM AT THE
LOWEST PRICES.

MRS. A. B. SMITH,
DEALER IN
Millinery & Straw Goods,
SILKS, RIBBONS, VELVETS,
CRAPES, LACES, &c., &c.,
124 State Street,
CHICAGO.

SIMEON W. KING,
Attorney-at-Law, Notary Public,
UNITED STATES COMMISSIONER,
And the only duly authorized
COMMISSIONER OF DEEDS
In Chicago, or the West, for *all* the *States* and *Territories*.
Office, No. 117 South Clark Street,
CHICAGO, ILLINOIS.

N B.—Passports Obtained, Marine Protests Entered, and Insurance Statements Certified to for *any* State or Territory.

CHICAGO IN 1830.

A SUCCESS

Without Parallel. — **In Mechanic Arts**

WILLCOX & GIBBS' SILENT FAMILY SEWING MACHINE.

A Few More — **Agents Wanted.**

WILLCOX & GIBBS SEWING MACHINE,

The Champion of 136 first premiums in two seasons. "Its seam is stronger and less liable to rip than the Lock Stitch."— *"Judges' Report of the Grand Trial."*

Send for the "Report," and Samples of work, containing both kinds of stitches on the same piece of goods. Agents wanted.

L. CORNELL & CO., Gen'l Agents,
133 Lake St., Chicago.

The Business of Chicago,

So large and so important, reaching in monopoly over a territory larger than the entire New England States, and largely connected with the trade and commerce of every known country in the world, has no success more complete or emphatic in its history than that of

WILLCOX & GIBBS'
SILENT SEWING MACHINE.

The Proprietors, L. CORNELL & CO., have for years stood among the most prudent, careful, and successful of our leading business men, and their position and enterprise, together with the greatest favor with which their famous Sewing Machine is everywhere received, identify them largely with the prosperity, history, and growth of Chicago. The name of their machine is a household word in every civilized part of the world, and no machine or firm is probably more favorably and widely known throughout the entire West, than the **Willcox & Gibbs' Sewing Machine** and **L. Cornell & Co.**, whose success is mainly due to the great merit of their goods and the high position won by uniform courtesy, integrity, candor, and honor, which characterize so many of our prominent business men.

A GUIDE

TO THE

CITY OF CHICAGO:

ITS

PUBLIC BUILDINGS, PLACES OF AMUSEMENT, COMMERCIAL, BENEVOLENT, AND RELIGIOUS INSTITUTIONS; CHURCHES, HOTELS, RAILROADS, ETC., ETC.

WITH A

MAP OF THE CITY,

AND

Numerous Illustrations of the Principal Buildings.

CHICAGO:
T. ELLWOOD ZELL & CO.
117 South Clark Street.
1868.

Entered according to Act of Congress, in the year 1867, by

T. ELLWOOD ZELL & CO.,

in the Clerk's Office of the District Court of the United States for the Northern District of Illinois.

The Little Corporal.

THE BEAUTIFUL CHROMO
"LITTLE RED RIDINGHOOD AND THE WOLF,"
AND OTHER
MAGNIFICENT PREMIUMS
ARE GIVEN FOR CLUBS.

ALFRED L. SEWELL,
Publisher of THE LITTLE CORPORAL,
Chicago, Ill.

AGENTS WANTED!

In every County and Town in the United States, to Canvass for the sale of the Finest and most Popular Oil-Print ever offered for sale in this Country.

A BEAUTIFUL CHROMO OF
BEARD'S GREAT PAINTING OF
"RED RIDINGHOOD
AND THE WOLF."

Large Profits can be made.

Price of Picture, $8 to $10, according to style of mounting.

For particulars, address

ALFRED L. SEWELL, Publisher,
Office, 138 Lake Street.   CHICAGO.

PROVIDENT
INSURANCE COMPANY
OF CHICAGO, ILL.
DEARBORN STREET, (Masonic Building.)

CAPITAL . . . . $1,000,000.
CHARTER PERPETUAL.
LIFE INSURANCE
AND
INSURANCE AGAINST ACCIDENTS.

Officers.

President, IRA Y. MUNN. | Vice Pres. H. E. SARGENT.
Secretary, ... C. HOLLAND.

Directors.

G. F. HARDING, Attorney at Law.	SAMUEL HALE,
T. B. BLACKSTONE,	Of Hale & Ayer, Iron Merch's.
Pres't Chic. & St. Louis R. R. Co.	H. E. SARGENT,
JOHN T. LINDSAY,	Gen'l Agent Michigan Cent. R.R.
Attorney at Law, Peoria, Ill.	MATTHEW LAFLIN, Capitalist.
IRA Y. MUNN, Commiss. Merc't.	W. H. RAND, Chicago Tribune Co.
C. HOLLAND, Secretary.	DANIEL THOMPSON,
WM. H. FERRY,	Commission Merchant, and
Managing Director C. & N.W. R'y.	Sup't City Railway.
F. H. WINSTON, Attorney at Law.	

Finance Committee.
WM. H. RAND.   G. F. HARDING.   F. H. WINSTON.

Medical Examiners.
DR. R. M. ISHAM, | DR. R. LUDLAM,
Prof. of Operat. Surgery, Chic. Med. Col. | Prof. Hahnemann Med. Col., Chicago.

A WORD TO THE READER.

THE want of a Guide Book, such as the one here presented to the public, has been so long felt and so generally acknowledged, that an apology for the present work is quite unnecessary. The design of this work is not only to furnish the immense number of strangers who visit this metropolis of the Northwest with a complete Guide to the public institutions and objects of interest, for which this young city has already become so famous, but at the same time contains a vast amount of matter, useful and valuable, that recommends it to the citizen as well as stranger. A glance at the Table of Contents will say more in its favor than can be said by the recommendation of the publisher.

A WORD TO THE READER.

We have also thought it proper to incorporate in this Strangers' Hand-Book the names of a few of our *first-class houses* in the various lines of trade, thereby rendering it a complete guide in this respect. The location of the stores may readily be found by consulting the Business Index.

THE WESTERN RURAL,

An Illustrated, Double-Quarto, Agricultural, Horticultural, and Family Weekly.

H. N. F. LEWIS,
EDITOR AND PUBLISHER.

WITH AN EFFICIENT CORPS OF ASSISTANTS AND CONTRIBUTORS,

84 AND 86 DEARBORN STREET,
Between Randolph and Washington Streets.

The Sixth Volume of this excellent and most successful Weekly commenced January 1, 1868. It has met a remarkable success, but not more than its real merits deserve. It is devoted mainly to Rural affairs, but gives also a great variety of Family Reading, choice original and selected Stories, and has a "Children's Corner" full of nice things for the little ones, a valuable department for the Ladies, etc. The market reports are a leading feature.

Its success is a striking example of Western growth and the result of well-directed enterprise. By liberally advertising its merits, and by remarkably generous gifts of premiums to those who raise clubs of subscribers, the Publisher has already secured for it a circulation *more than twice as large as any other Journal of its class west of New York!* During the year 1867 he gave away over $12,000 worth of Sewing-Machines alone. The Premium List embraces not only Sewing-Machines, the Wheeler & Wilson, Wilcox & Gibbs, and Howe, but a large variety of other highly desirable premiums for clubs of various sizes.

Residents and Visitors are invited to call at the Business Office, and Editorial and Printing Rooms, at 84 and 86 Dearborn Street, and make themselves known and receive specimen copies (*free*) for their own use, or to send to **friends** East or West.

The terms of subscription are $2.50 per year, and only $2.00 in clubs of four or more.

A. H. MILLER,
S. E. CORNER OF RANDOLPH AND CLARK STREETS,
CHICAGO,
And 132 Broadway, New York.

Manufacturer and Importer of

Watches,

Diamonds,

Gold Jewelry,

Silver Ware,

Plated Ware

Table Cutlery,

Marble Clocks,

Bronze Statuary,

Opera Glasses,

Fans, Canes,

Masonic Jewelry,

Writing Desks,

Travelers' Cases,

Musical Boxes,

And Presentation Goods of Every Description.
AGENT FOR THE CELEBRATED WATCHES OF
PATEK PHILIPPE & CO., GENEVA.

Diamonds, Precious Gems, and all kinds of Jewelry mounted and made to order in my own Factory over the Store.

☞ Particular attention given to the regulating and repairing of Fine Watches and Jewelry.

As this is one of the most beautiful stores in the country, I cordially invite strangers, as well as residents in the city, to inspect the goods on both the first and second floors of the house, assuring them that a visit will not incur the least obligation to purchase. A. H. MILLER.

CONTENTS.

	PAGE
ARTESIAN WELLS	66
Academy of Sciences	88
Athens Marble	72
Arlington Hall	125
Banks	128
Boards	128
Chamber of Commerce	80
Cemeteries	152
Catholic Asylum for Boys	101
Court House	83
Churches	146
Crosby Opera House	121
Cook County Hospital	107
Christian Association Library	112
Chicago	31
Chicago Orphan Asylum	98
" Historical Society	91
" Medical College	104
" Law Library	112
" Theological Seminary	85
" Eye and Ear Infirmary	102

CONTENTS.

	PAGE
Dearborn Observatory	85
" Park	119
Dispensaries	111
Douglas Monument	79
Erring Woman's Refuge	96
Fire Department	127
German Theatre	125
Hacks and Carriages	177
Half Orphan Asylum	101
Hotels	132
Home for the Friendless	95
Hospitals	107
Jewish Hospital	108
Jefferson Park	120
Lake Tunnel	62
" Hospital	108
" Park	120
Libraries and Reading-Rooms	111
Lincoln Park	119
Magdalen Asylum	
Mercy Hospital	107
McVicker's Theatre	122
Newspapers	141
Nicholson Pavement	75
Old Ladies' Home	97
Places of Entertainment	121
Presbyterian Theological Seminary	86
Police Department	12
Post-Office	126

M. POLACHEK,
Practical and Scientific
OPTICIAN,

45 South Clark Street, Chicago, Illinois.

The largest and most select assortment of Optical Goods of every description in the Northwest.

Orders from the Country, either in Wholesale or Retail, promptly filled.

VALUABLE SCHOOL BOOKS.

BLAIR'S RHETORIC & BELLE LETTRES.
LOCKE ON THE UNDERSTANDING

COLLOT'S FRENCH SERIES
CONSISTING OF

Collot's French Pronouncing Reader,
Collot's French Anecdotes and Questions,
Collot's French Dialogues and Phrases,
Collot's Interlinear French Reader,
Collot's Levizac's French Grammar.
Collot's Key to   do.   do.

Published by
T. ELLWOOD ZELL & CO.,
17 & 19 S. Sixth St. Phila.

THE Northwestern Presbyterian,

AS SUCCESSOR TO
PRESBYTERIAN STANDARD
AND
PRESBYTERIAN EXPOSITOR,
IS OUT IN
ENLARGED QUARTO FORM
AND NEW DRESS.

FOR 1868,

It will enter on its Eleventh Volume, in its present enlarged form, as an eight-page paper of the largest class, embracing, along with its RELIGIOUS DEPARTMENT, one of AGRICULTURE; one of the fullest and most reliable MONETARY, COMMERCIAL, and MARKET RECORDS; REVIEWS OF THE WEEK and of NEW PUBLICATIONS; able current EDITORIALS, on both the Religious and Miscellaneous pages; with a broad range of choice selected matter; articles from first-class contributors and correspondents in all parts of the world, including a live weekly letter from Washington. In breadth and completeness, the

NORTHWESTERN PRESBYTERIAN

is believed to be unsurpassed in American Journalism. Its programme for 1868 includes more enterprise, more comprehensiveness, and larger outlays, every way, than ever before.

$2.50 PER YEAR, IN ADVANCE.

To clubs of five, $2.00 each. Send for a specimen number.

Merchants and others will consult their own interests by advertising in the *Northwestern Presbyterian*, which is the only Presbyterian paper published in the Northwest. Address

NORTHWESTERN PRESBYTERIAN,
Chicago, Illinois.

CONTENTS.

	PAGE
Public Halls	125
" Parks	114
" Schools	113
Railroads	152
" (Street)	173
" Distances	181
Roman Catholic Orphan Asylums	102
Reform School	102
Rush Medical College	103
Savings Banks	131
Steamboats	152
Soldiers' Home	92
Societies	112
Streets	61
St. Luke's Hospital	107
Stock Yards	69
Theatres	121
Telegraph Offices	132
To Travellers	184
University of Chicago	84
Union Park	120
Vernon Park	120
Washingtonian Home	95
Washington Park	121
Watering-Places	182
Wood's Museum	122
Young Men's Library	111
" " Christian Association	86

GREAT EASTERN TEA COMPANY.

TEAS,
COFFEES,
SPICES.

CHICAGO DEPOT:
77 West Madison St.

☞ Constantly on hand, a full stock of pure new crop of Teas, Coffees, and Spices, which are offered to the Country Trade, Hotel-Keepers, and Housekeepers generally, throughout the Northwest at New York prices, with freight only added.

☞ Orders from the country filled at wholesale rates.

☞ Do not send to New York for these goods when they can be had from Chicago for LESS MONEY, in Less Time, and with Less Trouble, Risk, and Expense.

☞ All goods warranted to give satisfaction. Special attention to Country Club orders. Address

Great Eastern Tea Company,
77 West Madison St., Chicago, Ill.

BUSINESS INDEX.

APOTHECARIES AND PHARMACEUTISTS.

	Page
George Buck	53
Bliss & Sharp	35

BANKERS.

Tyler, Ullman & Co.	129

BAG MANUFACTURERS.

Hart, Asten & Co.	73

BAKING POWDERS.

Raney's Peerless	50
Royal Baking Powder	77

BOOTS AND SHOES (Wholesale).

Phelps, Dodge & Co.	60
Whitney, Bros. & Co.	162

BOOTS AND SHOES (Retail).

L. Mannheimer	67
Wiswall & Co.	73
Peter Keller	68
Hermerdinger & Co.	106
S. & P. Florsheim	139

BOOKSELLERS.

Church & Goodman	89
Eldredge & Brother	189
Poe & Hitchcock	144
Street, Moore & Co.	195
T. Ellwood Zell	5, 19, 42, 186, 192

Business Index.

CARPETS.
	PAGE
Allen & Mackey	169
Joseph West	37

CARD ENGRAVERS.
John B. Wiggins	117

CARRIAGES AND SLEIGHS.
Daniel Brainard	45
Thomas H. Brown	4

COACH AND SADDLERY HARDWARE
Brigham, Goodyear & Hayes	58

CONFECTIONS (Manufacturer).
P. L. Garrity	78

CONCRETE PAVEMENT.
Chicago Concrete Paving Company	74

CLOTHING.
H. H. Husted	64

COMMISSIONER OF DEEDS.
Simeon W. King	6

CROCKERY AND GLASSWARE.
Derrick & Salt	74
Merrill & Hopkins	109
John D. Zernitz	139

DRY GOODS (Wholesale).
J. V. Farwell & Co.	102
Bowen, Whitman & Winslow	148
S. D. Haskell & Co.	41

DRY GOODS (Wholesale and Retail).
Cushing & Souder	54
Field, Leiter & Co.	169
Shoenfeld Bros.	186

Business Index.

DRUGGISTS AND CHEMISTS.
	PAGE
BLISS & SHARP	35
GEORGE BUCK	53

DYE WORKS.
AUGUST SCHWARZ	77

ELASTIC SPONGE.
WESTERN ELASTIC SPONGE COMPANY	190

FOREIGN AND DOMESTIC FRUITS
F. NEWHALL & BROTHER	68
H. C. CHAMPION & CO.	109

FOREIGN & DOMESTIC LIQUORS.
A. RANNEY	124

FIRE INSURANCE.
GIRARD FIRE INS. CO.	191

FIRE-PROOF SAFES.
MAYNARD BROTHERS	170
HALL'S SAFE & LOCK COMPANY	136

FURNITURE.
JOHNSON & COBB	59
STEUER & ROBINSON	57

HARDWARE.
MILLER BROTHERS & KEEP	32
T. B. & H. M. SEAVEY	123
J. K. TYLER	134

HATTERS AND FURRIERS.
KLOKKE & HAND	139

HAT MANUFACTURERS.
LAMBERSON & BROTHER	82

HOSIERY AND GLOVES.
SEYMOUR, CARTER & CO.	2

Business Index.

HORTICULTURAL AND SEED WAREHOUSE.
	PAGE
Hovey & Nichols	86

HOOP SKIRTS.
Bean, Brownson & Co.	6

IVORY GOODS.
G. G. Thomas	37

JEWELRY AND SILVER WARE.
A. H. Miller	16
W. H. C. Miller	93
Giles Brother & Co.	105

LANDS.
Illinois Central R. R. Land Dep.	30

LAUNDRY.
State Street Laundry	123

LAMPS AND GLASSWARE.
E. F. Slocum	100

LIFE INSURANCE.
New York Life Insurance Company	140
Atlantic " " "	180
Economical " " "	90
Excelsior " " "	124
Provident " " "	12
Union " " "	109
Universal " " "	185
United States " "	42

MILLINERY GOODS (Wholesale).
D. B. Fisk & Co.	158

MILLINERS.
Mrs. A. B. Smith	6

MACHINERY.
R. M. Peare	77

Business Index.

MOWERS AND REAPERS.
	PAGE
E. Ball & Co.	130

MOVEMENT CURE.
Drs. J. G. & T. H. Trine	3

MUSIC PUBLISHERS.
De Motte Brothers	63
Root & Cady	150

MUSICAL INSTRUMENTS.
Root & Cady	150
De Motte Brothers	63

NEWSPAPERS.
N. W. Presbyterian	20
The Advance	143
New Republic	194
N. W. Christian Advocate	144
Irish Republic	46
New Covenant	153
Chicago Times	179
Western Rural	15
Little Corporal	11
Philadelphia Press	100

OPTICIANS.
M. Polachek	19
Dr. J. Phillips	4

PAPER MANUFACTURERS.
Charles Magarge & Co.	193

PAINTS AND OILS.
Hookers & Co.	45

PRINTERS.
Church, Goodman & Donnelly	89
Sherman & Co.	192

Business Index.

PRODUCE COMMISSION MERCHANTS.
	PAGE
Smith & Dexter	82
Caven & Perley	186
Charles Leeds & Co.	110

PRESERVED FRUITS.
Numsen, Carroll & Co.	99

PHOTOGRAPHERS.
S. M. Fassett	81

RESTAURANTS.
J. Wright (Opera House)	116

RAILROADS.
Illinois Central	94
Michigan Southern & Nor. Ind.	154

READY-MADE HOUSES.
Lyman Bridges	106

SAVINGS BANKS.
The Merchants, Farmers & Mechanics'	120

SCALES.
Fairbanks, Greenleaf & Co.	70

SCHOOL FURNITURE.
H. M. Sherwood	117

SEWING MACHINES.
Grover & Baker S. M. Co.	36
Wheeler & Wilson	76
Wilcox & Gibbs	7, 8
Empire	115

SEWING-SILKS (Jobbers).
Belding Brothers & Co.	3

SHIP CHANDLERS.
Gilbert Hubbard & Co.	174

Business Index.

SHOW-CASES.
	PAGE
D. Barclay	106
Vredenburgh Brothers	67

SILVER WARE.
N. W. Silver Ware Company	49

SMOKED MEATS.
Stiles, Goldy & McMahan	38
L. M. Prentiss & Co.	118

SPRING BEDS.
Empire Spring Bed Company	189

STEREOTYPE FOUNDERS.
John Fagan & Son	191

STOVES AND TINNERS' GOODS.
Seavey & Co.	38

SURGICAL INSTRUMENTS.
Bliss & Sharp	35

TEAS, COFFEES, SPICES.
Great Eastern Tea Company	22
American Tea House	5

TELEGRAPH COLLEGE.
Porter's College	133

TOILET GOODS.
Bliss & Sharp	35
George Buck	53

TURKISH BATHS.
Dr. John Wingrave	110

WOOD ENGRAVERS.
Maas & Manz	118
W. D. Baker	110
A. Marks	130

EIGHT HUNDRED THOUSAND ACRES OF
FARMING AND FRUIT LANDS
For Sale by the Illinois Central Railroad Company.

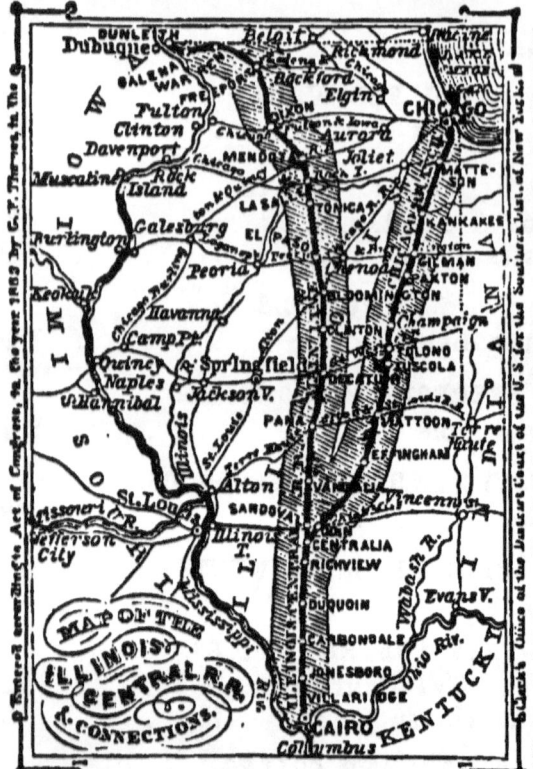

A considerable portion of these lands lie on the Chicago Branch of the Illinois Central Railroad, south from Chicago from 60 to 149 miles, in the centre of the corn belt and most favored climate, where the range for grazing is extensive, and healthful water from artesian wells readily obtained at a small expense, and direct railroad communication with the great markets of Chicago and Cairo. For Grain of all kinds, and stock raising, these lands are unsurpassed. Sheep thrive well, requiring fodder but a short season, and cheese factories are being successfully established along the entire line.

FRUIT GROWING

In Southern Illinois, is very profitable. A crop here seldom if ever fails. The early ripening of fruit enables the grower to command the high prices of the first of the season in all the Northern country. A Special Fruit Express Train runs to Chicago during the Fruit Season, and over 1,000,000 boxes of peaches, besides large quantities of berries and other fruits, were shipped to the Northern markets from the gardens and orchards of Egypt in 1867.

The lands of the Company are now offered at from $7 to $12 dollars per acre, with some few tracts at higher figures, rated according to quality and nearness to stations, and are sold on credit or for cash. A deduction of 10 per cent. from the credit price is made to those who purchase for cash.

☞ All Station Agents on the line are provided with plats, showing the lands for sale in their vicinity. Persons coming through Chicago can call at the office in the Land Department building, 58 Michigan Avenue, opposite the Great Central Depot, where prices and full information upon all points will be furnished, together with maps showing the exact locality of all the lands, or address, by letter, in any language, for the same, to

JOHN B. CALHOUN, Land Commissioner,
Illinois Central Railroad Co., CHICAGO, ILL.

GUIDE

TO THE

CITY OF CHICAGO.

CHICAGO.

Chicago is the largest and most important city in the Northwest, and, in its rapid growth, the most remarkable in the Union.

It is said that when Professor Goldwin Smith was preparing for his voyage to the United States, Mr. Richard Cobden said to him: "See two things in the United States, if nothing else,—Niagara and Chicago." The Professor acted upon this advice, and, while visiting this city, acknowledged that the two objects named by his friend were truly the greatest wonders of North America. According to geologists, the cataract has been about four thousand years in becoming what it is; but the city has come to its present growth in thirty-four years.

On a certain morning in the fall of the

year 1834, word was brought to the people of Chicago that a large black bear had been seen in a piece of woods a short distance out of town. The population capable of bearing arms, seized their guns and made for the forest, where the bear was soon shot. After so cheering an exploit, the hunters, disinclined to resume their ordinary labors, resolved to make a day of it, and have a dash at the wolves which then prowled nightly in every part of Chicago. Before night closed in, they had killed over forty wolves, all on the site of the present metropolis of the Northwest! The wolves did not take the hint, for we learn that, as late as 1838, the howlings of these pests of the prairies have been heard far within the present city limits.

In 1830, Chicago was what it had been for a quarter of a century,—a military post and fur station, consisting of twelve habitations. There was a log fort, with its garrison of two companies of United States troops; there was the fur agency; there were three taverns, so called, much visited by idle, drunken Indians, who brought in furs, and remained to drink up the proceeds; there were two stores, a blacksmith's shop, a house for the interpreter of the station, and one occupied by Indian chiefs. In 1831, there were

twelve families; and when winter came on, the troops having been withdrawn, the *whole population* moved into the fort, and had a pleasant time of it, with their debating society and balls. In 1832, the taxes amounted to one hundred and fifty dollars, twelve of which were expended in the erection of Chicago's first public building,—a pound for stray cattle.

But in 1833 the rush began. Before that year closed, there were fifty families in Chicago. When the forty wolves were slain, in 1834, there were, as it appears, nearly two thousand inhabitants in the town; and in 1835, more than three thousand.

Chicago, for fifteen years after it began its rapid increase, was perhaps of all prairie towns the most repulsive to every human sense. The place was in vile odor even among the Indians, since the name they gave it,—She-kaw-go,—if it does not mean skunk, as some aver, signifies nothing of sweeter odor than wild onion.

The prairie, on that part of the shore of Lake Michigan where the city stands, appears to the eye as flat as the lake itself, and its average height above the lake is about six feet. A gentleman who arrived at Chicago in 1833, reports that he waded the last eight miles of his journey in water from one to three feet deep,—a sheet of water extending as far as the eye could reach, over what is now the fashionable portion of the city. Another traveller remarked about the same time, that he "would not give sixpence an acre" for what is now the business portion of the city; some of which—corner of Clark and Lake streets—has recently been sold for *three thousand dollars per foot.*

Why settle such a spot, when better sites upon the same shore might have been selected? It was only because the Chicago River furnished the possibility of a harbor on the coast of the stormiest of lakes.

This Chicago River may not properly be termed a river, as the lake at this point cut into the soft prairie two hundred and fifty feet wide for a quarter of a mile, and then divided into two forks, one running south, the other north, both parallel with the lake-shore. There is no tide or flow to this curious inlet, except such as caused by the winds blowing the waters of the lake into it, which flows out when the wind changes or subsides. Originally this river was twenty feet deep, and being obstructed at its mouth by a sand-bar, it only admitted vessels of thirty or forty tons. But by dredging it has

TOILET GOODS.

TRAVELERS in need of anything in the line of FINE TOILET GOODS, will find a large and complete assortment of the VERY BEST GOODS at

BLISS & SHARP'S,

DRUGGISTS AND CHEMISTS,

144 LAKE STREET,

(Between CLARK and LA SALLE,)

CHICAGO.

Hair, Nail and Tooth Brushes; Shell, Ivory and Buffalo Combs; Colognes, Perfumery, Fine Soaps, Pomades, Cosmetics, Sponges, Hair Washes, Hand Mirrors, Rodgers' Cutlery and Scissors, Fine Purses of Russia Leather, Bath Brushes, Towels, Flasks, &c., &c.

BLISS & SHARP ARE AGENTS

for the sale of

GEO. TIEMANN & CO'S CELEBRATED

SURGICAL INSTRUMENTS,

and keep constantly on hand a full assortment.

SEWING MACHINES
AT THE
PARIS EXPOSITION.

"There seems to be considerable contradiction among the successful exhibitors as to the awards made in this department. The recipients of the two gold medals severally advertise that theirs is the only gold medal, thus contradicting each other, while all the other prize-holders concur that no gold medal was awarded to any sewing machine whatever. Happily, it is not our duty to decide this knotty question; but, be it as it may, the Grover and Baker Sewing Machines have received the very highest prize—above all medals—their representative in Paris having been decorated by the Emperor with the Cross of the Legion of Honor."

It is gratifying to find that the Grover and Baker Machine, which stands so high at home, should also receive the highest honor abroad. When it is remembered that one thousand gold medals were awarded at the Exposition, and only 150 decorations, it will be seen that the Cross of the Legion of Honor was considered by the judges as a much higher award of merit than the gold medal. No other sewing machine at the Exposition received this distinction, showing that, in the opinion of his Imperial Majesty, and the judges, no other was equally deserving. This award places the Grover & Baker Machine first in order on the official catalogue of the Exposition, as it is first in the estimation of the public on both sides of the Atlantic.

New York Express.

This is *the only* Company who make both *Double Lock Elastic Stitch*, and the Shuttle or *Lock Stitch* Machines; thus enabling parties to make selection and fair and impartial comparison. This Company make machines of both stitches, for all purposes of manufacturing and family use.

Their Machines have taken first-highest premiums throughout the world.

GENERAL NORTHWESTERN AGENCY,
104 & 106 Washington Street, Chicago, Ill.

AGENTS WANTED.— Liberal inducements offered to competent and responsible parties. Every one is invited to examine and test the Machines, and examine the great variety of work which these Machines are daily doing at the sales-room of the Company.

R. Wheeler, Agent.

CHICAGO IN 1868.

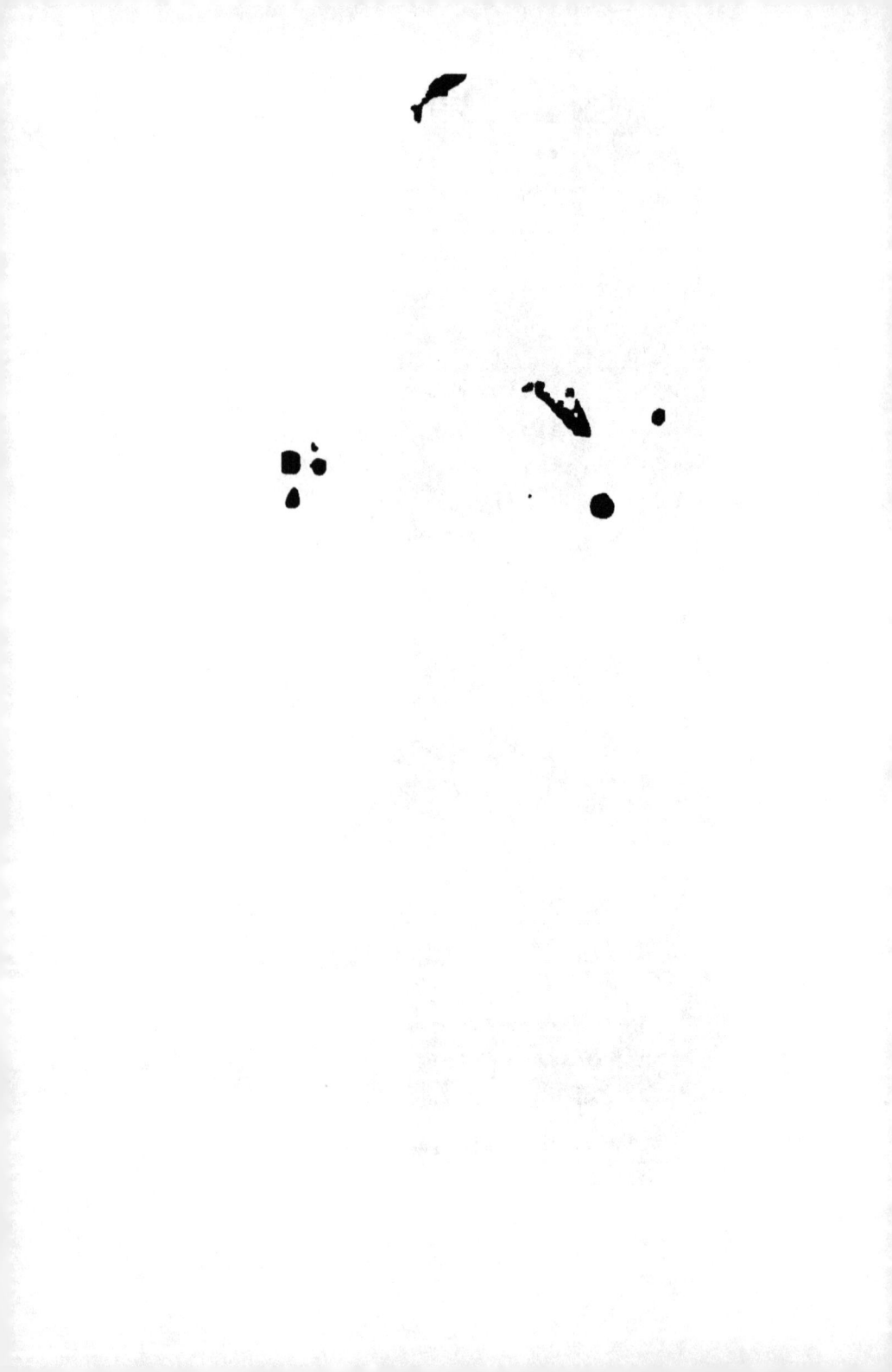

JOSEPH WEST,

70 Lake Street, Chicago, Illinois,

IMPORTER AND DEALER IN

English & American
CARPETING,

Matting, Oil Cloths, Druggets,
Rugs, Mats, Curtain Goods, &c.

PRIME FEATHERS.

G. G. THOMAS,
TURNER AND DEALER IN IVORY,
63 Clark St., Chicago, (opposite Sherman House.)

BILLIARD, BAGATELLE & POOL BALLS,
Ten-Pin Balls and Pins; Faro, Poker, and Eating-House Checks of all Patterns.

Fancy Carved
IVORY JEWELRY
in great variety.

All kinds of
IVORY GOODS, CANE TRIMMING, of all patterns, constantly on hand, or made to order.

— ALSO, —
Fancy and Plain
CUES,
CUE LEATHERS,
Improved
CUE CUTTERS
and
PRESSES,

Chalk, Pockets, Brushes, Cement & Stain,
WITH FULL DIRECTIONS FOR USE.

☞ *Balls Re-turned and Stained.*

STILES, GOLDY, & McMAHAN,
COMMISSION MERCHANTS
AND
𝔚holesale 𝔓rovision 𝔇ealers,
235 S. Water St., Chicago, Ill.

JOSIAH STILES,   OLIVER McMAHAN,
PERLEY G. STILES.   ISAIAH GOLDY.

Special attention given to the purchase and sale of provisions.

A large Stock of Beef and Pork Products constantly on hand.

E. D. SEAVEY.   D. H. SEAVEY.

SEAVEY & CO.,
Manufacturers of and Dealers in

TINNERS'
FURNISHING GOODS,
FRENCH ENAMELLED
AND
JAPANNED WARE,

Tin Plates, Sheet Iron, Coal Hods, Shovels, &c.

COOKING AND PARLOR STOVES,
HOT-AIR FURNACES.
No. 195 Lake St., Chicago.

been made capable of receiving the largest vessels that sail the lakes, and given to the city over thirty miles of wharves. Considering the peculiar destiny of Chicago, as the great distributer of commodities, no engineer could have contrived a more convenient harbor; for, go where you will in the city, you cannot get far from it, and every mill, warehouse, elevator, and factory, can have its branch, or basin, and receive or send away merchandise at its door. The drawbridges are a very serious obstacle at present; but there is a good prospect of overcoming this by tunnelling the river at various points. A tunnel is now in course of construction at Washington Street, at a cost of about one million dollars. In a very short time, these various draw-bridges will be superseded by as many tunnels.

Into this forked inlet, called a river, all the drainage of the city is poured, and there is no current to carry it away into the lake. Despite incessant dredging, these streams of impurity fill the channel, and converts the water into a filthy state. This great evil is being overcome. The Board of Public Works are now expending three millions of dollars in changing this pool of abominations into a pure and running stream. The canal which connects Lake Michigan with the Illinois River, begins at one of the branches of the Chicago River, the water of which is now pumped up into the canal by steam. This canal is being deepened, so that the water of the river will flow into it, and run down through all its length to the Illinois, and so carry away the impurities of the city to the Mississippi. Thus, by one operation, the pumping is obviated, the canal is improved, the river is purified, and the city is rendered more healthy. The Chicago River, therefore, will at length become a river, only it will run backwards.

The growth of Chicago, since 1833, strikes every mind with wonder and astonishment. The mystery, however, may in a measure be solved in considering the location of the city. Standing as it does at the southern end of Lake Michigan, gives it necessarily a leading share of the commerce of all the lakes, and easy access by land, round the southern shore of Lake Michigan, to all the East and Southeast. Chicago might have continued as it was previous to 1833, if the region behind it had remained unpeopled. The city has grown with the development of the region round about, and has become its grand depot, exchange, counting-house, and metropolis.

S. D. HASKELL & Co.
DRY .GOODS
COMMISSION MERCHANTS,
23 & 25 Randolph St., Chicago.

AGENTS FOR THE SALE OF

Fletcher Manufacturing Co's Shoe Laces, Crochet Braids, Wicks, &c.
Dexter & Brothers' Superior Knitting Cotton.
D. Goff & Son's Crown Alpaca and Dress Braids.
Spicket Falls Braid Works' Alpaca Braids.
Greene Brothers' Welting Cord and Skein Cotton.
Stuart's "Standard" Shoe Thread.
Union Elastic Goods Co's Suspenders, &c.
C. & W's Shirts and Drawers, Wool Socks, Box and Pound Yarns.
Star Knitting Co's Shirts and Drawers (all kinds).
Syracuse Hosiery Co's Hosiery (Ladies & Gents).
D. & S's Fancy Worsted Goods, Hoods, Nubias, &c., &c.
New Hampshire Celebrated **Horse Blankets.**
Manchester 9-4, 10-4, and 11-4 Counterpanes.
Arkwright, Harris' and other Bleached Cottons, Sheetings, Corset Jeans, Apron Checks, Gingham Prints, and other Domestic Cotton Goods, all of which we offer, to the **Jobbing Trade only,** at New York Agents' **lowest** cash Prices. **Guaranteed**—subject to the addition of freight to Chicago. Also agents for
J. Scholfield's (Constantine, Mich.) "Red Line" Cassimeres, Flannels and Blankets.

☞ We desire an acquaintance with **WESTERN MANUFACTURERS.**

THE UNITED STATES LIFE INSURANCE COMPANY

OF NEW YORK.

Organized A.D. 1850.

Cash Assets, $2,400,000.

Branch Office:

Room 8, Mercantile Block, 116 La Salle Street, Chicago, Ill.

JAS. F. BRADLEY, General Agent,
FRED. S. POND, Special Agent

for Northern Illinois and Wisconsin.

POPULAR POETS.

Published by

T. ELLWOOD ZELL & Co.,

Philadelphia, Pa.

Wordsworth Royal 8vo.
Hart's Spencer's Faerie Queene.
Milton's Paradise Lost.

POCKET EDITION OF

Pollock's Course of Time.
Young's Night Thoughts.
Tomson's Seasons.

Apply as above.

The crowds of idle and dissolute Indians were the first obstacle to the growth of Chicago, with which the early settlers had to contend. In 1833, seven thousand of them gathered at this point to meet the Commissioners of the United States for the purpose of selling their lands in Illinois and Wisconsin. The chiefs signed a treaty which ceded to the United States twenty million acres of the Northwest, and agreed to remove twenty days' journey west of the Mississippi River. A year later, four thousand of these dusky faces assembled in Chicago to receive their first annuity. The goods to be distributed were piled up on the prairie, and some of the red-skins becoming dissatisfied with the method of distribution, rushed upon the heap and attempted to seize something from it. So severe was the scramble, that a general fight was the result, in which several Indians were killed and many wounded. Night closed in on a wild debauch, and next morning few of the Indians were the better off for the thirty thousand dollars' worth of goods which had been given to them. Similar scenes, with similar bloody results, were enacted in the fall of 1835; but that was the last Indian payment Chicago witnessed. In September, 1835, a long train of fifty wagons, drawn by oxen, conveyed away, across the prairies, the Indians and their effects. In twenty days they crossed the Mississippi, and for twenty days longer continued their westward march, and Chicago was troubled with them no more. Walking in the imposing streets of the city of Chicago to-day, how difficult it is to realize that thirty-three years have not elapsed since the red men were dispossessed of the very site on which the city stands, and that it required forty days to carry them to a point now reached in fifteen hours.

In 1836, the population of the city was four thousand. Then there was a check to its prosperity, as to that of Illinois and the United States, and the population scarcely increased for five years. But it was in those very years of depression and despair that Chicago entered upon a new career. A little beef had been salted and sent across the lake; but in 1839 the business began to assume promising proportions; 3000 cattle were driven in from the prairie, cut, packed, and exported. Since that time the packing business has continued to increase with the growth of the city, and the development of the great West. The following figures, showing the number of cattle packed in the city

D. BRAINARD,
DEALER IN FIRST CLASS

Carriages, Light Buggies and Sleighs,
REPOSITORY, 187 STATE STREET,
CHICAGO, ILL.

We have all the latest styles of top and open Buggies, Family Carriages, such as the English Park Phaetons. Rockaways, Cabriolets, Victorias, and Slide Seats. Also, Hearses.

HOOKERS & CO.,

127 SOUTH WATER STREET,

Wholesale Dealers in

PAINTS, OILS,
VARNISHES,
Window-Glass,
BRUSHES, &c.

FAYETTE HOOKER.   HENRY M. HOOKER.   JOHN F. WEARE.

THE IRISH REPUBLIC;

A JOURNAL DEVOTED TO

Liberty, Literature, and Social Progress.

It will be "Independent in all things; Neutral in nothing."

The want of such an organ of truly liberal principles has been widely and deeply felt, especially among Irishmen of advanced opinions, and among the real friends of Irish national independence and of universal liberty. By the corrupt, or incompetent, organs of parties and sects, the Irish people of this country have, up to a very late period, been at once misrepresented and misled. It is time that this was at an end; and that the true advocates of liberty to Ireland, and to all men, should come forward as the real representatives of their race and nation, and make the truth manifest to the entire intelligent world, that, while we demand justice for ourselves, we are ready and anxious to extend it to all others.

Rates of Subscription for the Irish Republic.

Single copies for one year, ... $5 00
Single copies for six months, ... 2 50

Clubs.

Five copies to one address, one year, ... 22 50
Ten copies to one address, one year, ... 40 00
Twenty copies to one address, one year, ... 70 00
Thirty copies to one address, one year, ... 90 00

It is thus evident that a club of 30 members can have the paper at the rate of $3 a year for each member.

The most liberal allowances made to Agents, who can find profitable employment, but who must give the most undoubted reference as to ability, integrity, and business qualifications. The indorsement of any Circle, or its officers in good standing, will be sufficient.

Office of the IRISH REPUBLIC,
84 *Washington Street,*
P. O. Drawer 5900. *Chicago, Ill.*

during the last seventeen years, will give a correct idea of the growth of the trade: —

1851	21,900	1859	52,340
1852	25,400	1860	33,976
1853	24,820	1861	54,629
1854	23,987	1862	60,428
1855	27,729	1863	72,120
1856	25,870	1864	93,724
1857	35,400	1865	99,864
1858	44,700	1866	121,320
		1867	127,210

The first shipment of grain from Chicago, of which there is any record, was made in 1838, when a rather venturesome trader sent off *seventy-eight* bushels of wheat. The following year over four thousand bushels were exported, in 1848 over three millions, and in 1867 *thirteen million bushels.* During 1867 there were shipped from Chicago 27,000,000 bushels corn, 18,000,000 bushels oats, 2,200,000 bushels rye, and 1,700,000 bushels barley. Thus it may be seen what a gigantic business the grain trade has become. The ease, the celerity, and quietness with which this immense quantity of grain is handled, although hands never touch it, is one of the wonders of Chicago. Whether it arrives by boat or railroad, it comes in bulk, that is, loose, without bags or barrels. The car or boat stops at the side of one of the twenty-two elevators within the city, by which the grain is pumped into enormous bins, and poured out into other cars or vessels on the other side of the building,—the double operation being performed by steam in a few minutes. When Chicago exported a few thousand bushels a year, the business blocked the streets and filled the place with commotion; but now that it exports fifty million bushels, a person might live a year in the city without being aware that anything was doing in grain.

The business of pork-packing has also attained enormous proportions in Chicago, surpassing entirely Cincinnati, where it originated. In one season of three months, Chicago converted over one million hogs into pork; which was one-third of all the hogs slaughtered in the Western country during the year.

During the last few years the number of cattle received in Chicago from the prairies, and sent away in various forms to the East, has averaged about one thousand per day. Nevertheless a stranger in Chicago might never suspect that any business was done in cattle—never see a drove, never hear the bellow of an ox. All the business is done at the great Stock Yards, a description of which will be found ir this work.

N. W. Silver Ware Manufacturing Co.
OF CHICAGO.

FACTORY, COR. STATE STREET AND ELDRIDGE COURT.

Manufacturers of all kinds of

Solid Silver Goods
AND GOLD AND SILVER WATCH CASES.

OFFICERS.

P. H. WILLARD, ... President.   T. P. HART, ... Secretary.
A. D. TITSWORTH, . Vice-Pres.   L. J. GAGE, ... Treasurer.
Manager and Sup't, JAMES H. HOES, formerly of Matson & Hoes.

Gold and Silver Plating and Re-Plating Done on Short Notice.

P. O. Box 1954.

RANEY'S PEERLESS Baking Powder.

A. Raney & Co.
CHICAGO.

THIS POWDER
HAS NEVER BEEN EQUALLED AND CANNOT BE EXCELLED.

Wholesale dealers will find it to their interest to give us an order.

Chicago also stands foremost in the lumber business. Like the grain and cattle trade, it has developed itself into startling proportions. From thirty-three millions of feet received in Chicago, in 1847, it has increased until it reached, in 1867, the amount of *seven hundred and ninety-five millions of feet.* Miles upon miles of lumber-yards extend along the south fork of the river. The prairies, to which Nature has been so variously bountiful, lack this great necessity of the settler, and it is Chicago that sends up the lake for it, and supplies it to the prairies. To economize transportation, we are now beginning to dispatch timber in the form of ready-made houses. There is a firm in this city who are ready to furnish cottages, stores, churches, hotels, or towns, wholesale and retail, and to forward them securely packed to any part of the country.

Until within the last ten or twelve years, Chicago was little more than what it has been termed,—the great Northwestern Exchange. It was a buyer and seller on a grand scale; but it *made* scarcely anything, depending upon the Eastern States for supplies of manufactured merchandise. At the present time, almost every article of much bulk used upon railroads, in farming, in warming houses, in building houses, or in cooking, is made in Chicago. Four thousand persons are engaged in manufacturing boots and shoes. The prairies are now mowed by machines made in this city. A short distance from the city stands the Chicago Clock Factory, capable of manufacturing one hundred and fifty thousand clocks a year. Still farther back on the prairies is the National Watch Company, which soon expects to produce fifty watches a day. Pianos and melodeons are also made on a great scale in the city.

Chicago, already a handsome town, is going to be one of the most beautiful cities on the continent. It is no longer a quagmire. The mud and water for a long period were the despair of the people, since water will only run down-hill, and part of the town was below the level of the lake. Planking was a poor expedient, though unavoidable for a time. Open ditches were tried for a while, which in wet seasons only aggravated the difficulty. It became clear, at length, that nothing would suffice short of raising the whole town; and accordingly a higher grade was established, to which all new buildings were required to conform. It soon appeared that this grade was not high enough, and one still higher was ordered.

BUCK,
SUCCESSOR TO BUCK & RAYNER,
Apothecary and Pharmaceutist.

PURE DRUGS AND MEDICINES,
Selected and prepared expressly for our
SPECIAL PRESCRIPTION TRADE.

We devote attention *chiefly* to the preparation of Medicines and Physicians' Prescriptions, and keep constantly a large stock of the most reliable

MEDICINES, CHEMICALS, APPARATUS AND PHARMACEUTICAL PREPARATIONS,
of American and Foreign Manufacture.

CHOICE WINES AND LIQUORS,
— AND —
DELICACIES FOR INVALIDS, PURE COOKING ARTICLES, &c. &c.

We also have always on hand an extensive assortment of the

FINEST TOILET GOODS,
CONSISTING OF

Brushes, Combs, Perfumery, Pomades, Oils and Cosmetics of every description.

OUR SPLENDID MARBLE SODA FOUNTAIN
is in full operation between May 1st and October 1st of each year.

Open after the close of Public Amusements.

CENTRAL PRESCRIPTION DRUG STORE,
93 S. Clark St., (Larmon Block,)
CHICAGO.

CUSHING & SOUDER,

WHOLESALE & RETAIL DEALERS IN

Dry Goods & Notions.

NEW GOODS

Received Daily and sold at the

LOWEST CASH AUCTION PRICES,

AT THE

OLD STAND,

No. 73 Lake Street,

TREMONT HOUSE BLOCK,

CHICAGO,

ILLINOIS.

Even this proved inadequate; and the present grade was adopted, which lifts the city about twelve feet above the level of the prairie. All the new houses are built upon the new grade, and some old buildings have been raised to the proper level; but many houses are yet upon the grades previously established, and a large number are down upon the original prairie. The consequence is, that in some sections of the city the plank sidewalks are a series of stairs.

The principal streets are paved with that *ne plus ultra* of comfort for horse and rider,— the Nicholson pavement, a description of which will be found among the following pages.

Chicago is still a forming city. It stretches along the lake about eight miles, but does not reach back into the prairie more than three. Along the lake, south of the river, for two or three miles extend the beautiful avenues, which change insensibly into those streets of cottages and gardens which have given Chicago the name of the Garden City. This is a pleasant quarter, where glimpses are caught of the blue lake that stretches away to the east for sixty miles. On this shore is rising the monument to Douglas, and near by in shady retreats stands the Soldiers' Home, and Chicago University, a description of each of which we have devoted separate articles in the succeeding pages of this work.

It is always interesting to a stranger to notice the names of the streets of a city which he visits for the first time. We will therefore give a few of the quaint ones.

The city boasts of a Goethe street, a Schiller, a Greeley, a Poe, a Kane, a Kossuth, a Wentworth, and a Long John street. Local history is commemorated in Astor, Kinsie, Fur, Blackhawk, Calumet, and Wahpanseh; general history, in Blucher, Bonaparte, Macedonia, Garibaldi, Kansas, Mayflower, Fabius, and Sigel. There is also a Rosebud street, a Selah street, a Queer Place, and a Grub street.

The natural advantages of Chicago, together with the energy and perseverance of her citizens, have been the cause of the city's growth. The following table will show at a glance its rapid strides since it was only an outpost of civilization.

Population of Chicago from 1829 *to* 1867.

1829	35	1833	370
1830	49	1834	1,720
1831	73	1835	3,440
1832	428	1836	4,100

CHARLES STEUER.　　　　　　　W. LEACH ROBINSON.

FURNITURE.

Steuer and Robinson,

Manufacturers and Dealers in

FINE AND MEDIUM

FURNITURE.

ROSEWOOD, BLACK WALNUT, & MAHOGANY

PARLOR SUITES

In Reps, Haircloth, and Silk.

ROSEWOOD, WALNUT, CHESTNUT, & PAINTED

CHAMBER SETS.

A LARGE VARIETY OF FURNITURE

FOR EVERY ROOM IN THE HOUSE.

We make a specialty of manufacturing to order,

Fine Draperies, Parlor & Library Suites, &c.

STEUER & ROBINSON,
No. 190 Lake Street,
CHICAGO.

BRIGHAM, GOODYEAR & HAYES,

181 LAKE STREET,

CHICAGO, ILL.,

Wholesale Dealers in

COACH AND SADDLERY

HARDWARE,

Patent, Enameled, and Harness

LEATHER,

HUBS, SPOKES, BENT FELLOES,

And all other articles of Bent Carriage Work.

SPRINGS, AXLES, BOLTS, AND MALLEABLE IRON

Seward's Axle Clips, Philadelphia Bolts, Broad-cloths, Damask, Enameled Cloths, Muslin, Drill and Duck, Coach Laces of all kinds, Carpeting, Drugget, Moquette, Plush, Corduroy, and all kinds of Sleigh Trimmings, Curled Hair, Moss and Tow, Saddles and Collars, Horse Blankets, Lap Robes, Affghans, Fancy Work Mats, Leather and Linen Fly-Nets, Linen Horse-Sheets, &c. &c.

G. F. BRIGHAM.　　C. B. GOODYEAR.　　J. B. HAYES.

CHAMBER OF COMMERCE.
Chicago.

JOHNSON & COBB,

Manufacturers and Wholesale and Retail Dealers in

BEDDING

AND

FURNITURE,

152 STATE STREET,

Between Madison and Monroe.

CHAMBER SETS

Of all kinds on hand, and for sale at the very lowest figures.

A LARGE ASSORTMENT OF

Blankets, Feather Pillows, and Bolsters, Counterpanes, Sheets, Pillow Slips, &c.

ORDERS PROMPTLY FILLED

Our MATTRESSES made full and of good size.

JOHNSON & COBB,
CHICAGO.

PHELPS, DODGE & CO.,

MANUFACTURERS AND JOBBERS OF

Boots and Shoes,

50 Lake Street,

Would call the attention of purchasers to their large and complete stock of goods, embracing every style and quality required in the retail trade.

We wish particularly to mention our CELEBRATED P. D. & Co. WORK. Every shoe warranted. It has stood a four years' test, and pronounced by all, the best in style and material that can be found in the market.

OUR OWN MAKE CHICAGO BOOTS

Have borne the palm of superiority from all competitors, and we confidently claim for them

THE CHAMPIONSHIP OF THE NORTHWEST.

Our terms of warrantee are the most LIBERAL and comprehensive imaginable. In all cases when our boots have been sold, and a defect discovered by the purchaser, we instruct the dealer to furnish him a NEW PAIR, in place of the defective ones, and will consider it a favor to have them returned to us at our expense.

We cordially invite all CASH and prompt-paying purchasers to call and investigate the subject, believing it to be to their interest.

A GUIDE TO CHICAGO.

1837	4,349	1852	39,629
1838	4,220	1853	58,754
1839	4,440	1854	66,361
1840	4,370	1855	79,440
1841	5,650	1856	87,390
1842	6,800	1857	95,600
1843	7,950	1858	84,584
1844	8,300	1859	93,260
1845	12,210	1860	108,247
1846	14,756	1861	122,740
1847	16,420	1862	139,320
1848	21,200	1863	154,710
1849	23,628	1864	171,356
1850	28,347	1865	177,621
1851	35,200	1866	221,000

1867..................255,000.

STREETS.

The Lake is situate on the east side of the city. Michigan Avenue runs north and south, parallel with and along the lake-shore; next west of it is Wabash Avenue; then State, Dearborn, Clark, La Salle, Wells, Franklin, and Market Streets; west of Market Street and parallel with it is the south branch of the Chicago River. Running east and west along the south side of the main Chicago River, is South Water Street; next south of it is Lake Street, then Randolph, Washington, Madison, Monroe, Adams, Quincy, Jackson, Van Buren, Harrison, Polk, Twelfth, Thirteenth, and so

. on. These streets continue on the west side of the river, and are called West Randolph, West Washington, etc.

The West Division comprises all of the city west of both branches of the river, and those streets running north and south are divided by West Randolph Street. The North Division comprises that portion of the city north of the main river, and between the lake on the east, and the north-west branch. Those streets continued from the south side are called North Dearborn, North Clark, North La Salle, and so on.

By reference to the map, accompanying this work, the location of the streets may easily be found.

LAKE TUNNEL.

The Tunnel begins a short distance from Chicago Avenue, on the lake-shore, and extends two miles out under the lake in a straight line, at right angles to the general direction of the shore. The tunnel is very near circular in form, and has an interior width of five feet and a height of five feet two inches, enclosed in brick masonry eight inches thick. The depth of the shore-shaft, —which is eight feet in diameter, circular in

De Motte Brothers,

SUCCESSORS TO H. M. HIGGINS,

MUSIC PUBLISHERS.

WHOLESALE & RETAIL DEALERS IN

ALL KINDS OF

SHEET MUSIC BOOKS

AND

MUSICAL INSTRUMENTS.

Sole Agents for the

"WEBER" & "GUILD"

Pianofortes.

☞ Liberal Discounts made to Dealers and Teachers.

De MOTTE BROS.,
91 Washington St.,
CHICAGO.

139 & 141 RANDOLPH ST.,
SHERMAN HOUSE BUILDING,
Chicago, Ill.

CLOTHING

At Wholesale & Retail.

H. H. HUSTED

has a large and well selected stock of

CLOTHING & GENT'S FURNISHING GOODS.

The Goods have all been bought and manufactured since the large decline in WOOLLENS, and patrons may depend upon getting goods at the

LOWEST LIVING PRICES.

Merchants purchasing to sell again will always find some job lots that can be bought at very low prices.

—ALSO—

YOUTHS' AND CHILDREN'S CLOTHING.

In the

CUSTOM DEPARTMENT

Will be found a choice stock of Cloths, Cassimeres, and Vestings, which will be made to order at short notice.

H. H. HUSTED,
139 & 141 Randolph St.

form, and of brick masonry,—at the bottom of which the tunnel commences its direction out under the lake, is sixty-seven feet; and the depth of the lake-shaft, which is of cast iron, of the same dimensions as the shore-shaft, below the surface of the lake, sixty-four feet. This latter shaft is provided with gates to let on and shut off the water at pleasure.

To protect the lake-shaft from the fury of the gales that sweep from the prairies over the lake, a five-sided crib, (the location of which may be seen by reference to the map,) forty-five feet high and fifty-eight feet in width, was constructed, and placed in its present position in July, 1865. The depth of the lake at the crib is thirty-five feet, thus leaving the top of the crib ten feet above the ordinary surface of the lake. This crib, which is built of twelve-inch timber, consists of an outside, centre, and inside wall, each wall connected by cross timbers running entirely through from outside to inside, all securely fastened with square bolts. It is kept in its proper position by being filled with about twelve thousand tons of stone. There are three openings in the sides of the crib, by which the water is let in or shut off. Each of these flumes are five feet square. The first one is about five feet from the bottom of the lake; another ten feet; and the last fifteen feet, or thirty feet below the top of the crib, thus insuring the purest of water.

The work upon this gigantic enterprise was commenced in March, 1864, and completed in July, 1867. The contract price was $315,000, but through various causes it has cost about $800,000. It is a work that Chicago may be proud of, not especially for its magnitude, but for the simplicity, originality, and boldness of the idea.

Buildings of more than usual architectural beauty for the pumping-works have recently been erected on the corner of Chicago Avenue and Pine Street. These structures, together with their surrounding grounds, are pleasing in their appearance, and ornaments to the city.

THE ARTESIAN WELLS.

No stranger will fail to visit these objects of peculiar interest. They are located at the corner of Western and Chicago avenues, and may readily be reached by the Randolph-Street cars. There are two wells, one about seven hundred and the other about one thousand feet deep. These wells were first bored by some oil speculators, who were led

77 LAKE ST., 77 LAKE ST.,
Chicago, Ill.
L. MANNHEIMER,
BOOTS & SHOES.
A LARGE STOCK OF THE BEST GOODS CONSTANTLY KEPT ON HAND.

DEPOT FOR E. C. BURT'S
CELEBRATED BOOTS.

Having made these goods a specialty, I am enabled to sell them cheaper than any other house in the city.

VREDENBURGH BROS.

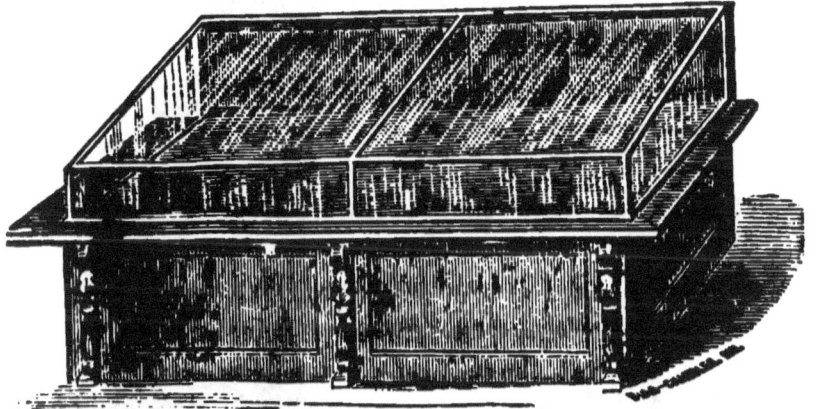

SHOWCASE WARE ROOMS,
151 & 153 *Randolph* St., (opposite Court House,) *Chicago.*

Show-Cases of every description and material, Silver, White Metal, and Wood, shipped to all parts of the United States. Parties will do well to call and examine our Metal Work, which is on an improved plan, and something new in style.

F. NEWHALL & BRO.,
WHOLESALE DEALERS IN
FOREIGN AND DOMESTIC GREEN, DRIED, AND CANNED

FRUITS,
NUTS AND FANCY GROCERIES.
6 DEARBORN STREET,
CHICAGO, ILL.

PACKERS AND JOBBERS OF
NEW YORK AND MICHIGAN APPLES.
CIDER BY THE BARREL.

PETER KELLER,
PREMIUM
Boot Maker,
41 La SALLE ST.,
Between Lake and Randolph,
CHICAGO.

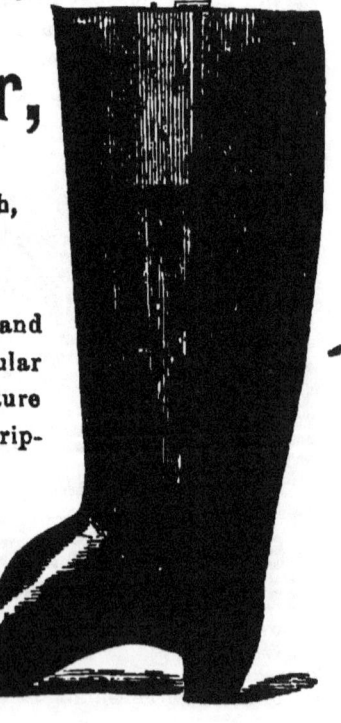

☞ Gentlemen's BOOTS and SHOES made to order. Particular attention given to the manufacture of Ladies' Boots of every description.

☞ A full assortment of every kind of Ladies' and Gentlemen's Boots always on hand and cheap for cash.

to the spot by a spiritual medium, who asserted that petroleum would be found in great quantities beneath the surface. But instead of oil, a very little of which appeared, water began to flow, and has continued to come forth at the rate of a million gallons a day. The two wells are very near together, and have bores of from five to six inches in diameter.

STOCK YARDS.

Out on the prairie, four miles south of the city, and two feet below the level of the river, may be seen the famous Stock Yards. Two millions of dollars have been expended there in the construction of a cattle-market. The company owning it have nearly a square mile of land, 355 acres of which are enclosed with cattle-pens,—150 of these acres being floored with plank. There is at the present time pen-room for 25,000 cattle, 80,000 hogs, and 25,000 sheep, the sheep and hogs being provided with sheds; and no Thursday has passed since the yards were opened, when they were not full,—Thursday being the full day, and the best time to visit the yards. This bovine city of the world, like most prairie cities, is laid out in streets and alleys crossing at right angles. The principal street is named Broadway. It is a mile long and seventy-five feet wide, and is divided by a light fence into three paths, so that herds of cattle can pass one another without mingling, and leave an unobstructed road for the drovers. Nine railroads have constructed branches to the yards, and there is also a canal connecting it with the Chicago River

Nothing is more simple and easy than the working of these stock yards. A cattle train stops along a street of pens; the side of each car is removed; a gently declining bridge wooes the living freight down into a clean, planked enclosure, where on one side is a long trough, which the turn of a faucet fills with water; and on another side is a manger, which can be immediately filled with hay. While the tired and hungry animals are enjoying this respite from the torture of their ride, their owner or his agent finds comfort in the Hough House, a handsome hotel of yellow stone, built solely for the accommodation of the cattle-men, and capable of entertaining two hundred of them at once. A few steps from the hotel is the Cattle Exchange, another spacious and elegant edifice, wherein there is a great

room for the chaffering or preliminary "gasing" of buyers and sellers; also a Bank, solely for cattle-men's use, with a daily business of from one hundred thousand to half a million dollars; also a telegraph office, which reports, from time to time, the price of beef, pork, and mutton in two hemispheres, and sends back to the cattle-markets of mankind the condition of affairs in this, the great bovine city of the world. The preliminaries being over, the cattle-men leave the Exchange, and go forth to view the cattle. The purchase completed, the cattle are driven along, through opening pens and broad streets, to the yards adjoining the railroad by which they are to resume their journey. On the way to those yards they are weighed at the rate of thirty cattle a minute, by merely pausing in the weighing-pen as they pass. The men return to the Exchange, where the money is paid,—all the cattle business being done for cash; after which they conclude the affair by dining together at the hotel.

In the elegant Exchange two classes of cattle-men are met,—those who collect the cattle from the prairie States, Texas, Missouri, Kansas, Iowa, Wisconsin, Minnesota,

Illinois, — and those who distribute the cattle among the Eastern cities.

The design of the directors of these yards is to keep the rent of these pens at such rates as to exactly pay the cost of cleaning and preserving them, and to get the requisite profit only from the sale of hay and corn. One hundred tons of hay are frequently used in the yards in one day. If these yards were in any of the Eastern States, the sale of the manure would be an important part of the business; but the fertile prairies not needing anything of the kind, they are glad to sell it at ten cents a wagon-load, which is less than the cost of shovelling it up.

These yards may be reached by the Archer Avenue line of street-cars, and the Pittsburg, Fort Wayne, and Chicago Railroad. As we have said before, Thursday is the day to visit the yards and see the pens full.

ATHENS MARBLE.

While the canal was being constructed at Athens, a point about sixteen miles from the city, a deposit of soft, cream-colored stone was discovered, which proved to be an inexhaustible quarry. For some time this stone

A Place ALL should Visit!
75 Lake Street, or 35 Clark Street.

Persons visiting the city should not fail to call at one of the Stores of

WISWALL & CO.,
DEALERS IN
FINE BOOTS AND SHOES
OF EVERY VARIETY.

Their stock is one of the largest and most complete of any in the city, and for durability and excellence cannot be surpassed.

We make a specialty of BURT'S GOODS for Ladies, Misses, and Children's wear.

Also, a full line of White Kid, Satin and Jean Gaiters and Slippers can be found here. Remember our numbers,

75 LAKE, or 35 CLARK STREET,
CHICAGO, ILL.

HART, ASTEN & CO.,
MANUFACTURERS OF AND DEALERS IN

FLOR SACKS,

Seamless BAGS,

GUNNY BAGS,

And BAGS of every description.

SOMETHING NEW!
CHICAGO CONCRETE PAVING CO.
For Pavements, Carriage-Ways, Walks, Docks, etc.
THE BURLEW AND FISK PATENTS

For Walks, Flagging, Pavement, and like purposes, have now been so thoroughly tested, that the proprietors confidently recommend them as without a superior in this country.

About two years ago a specimen was laid down in DRUID HILL PARK, Baltimore, Md., which has proved perfectly satisfactory; and a very large number has been laid in the Central Park and City Hall Park. in the City of New York, Prospect Hill Park, Brooklyn and vicinity; and Side Walks can now be seen in front of J. B. Taylor's residence, No. 749 Wabash Avenue; Dr. Bigelow, and others, in the immediate vicinity, in this city. Street Pavements will soon follow, and will produce a complete revolution in the Paving and Walks of this Emporium of the West.

Private Walks, Carriage-Ways, Docks, Street Pavements, Cellar Bottoms, Stable Floors, Vault Covers, &c., all attest to its superior qualities, and a thorough examination will show why it is preferable to any other material for these purposes. Its durability is equal to that of stone.

For further information in relation to the business, or for the laying of this kind of work. or for the purchase of Town, County, or State Rights, in the Northwestern States, apply to

A. RANNEY & CO., Proprietors,
At the principal Office of the Company,
No. 185 Kinzie Street, Revere House Block,
All Communications to be addressed to
FRANK W. CHAFFEE, Chicago, Ill.
Secretary and General Business Manager, at the above address.

DERRICK & SALT,
IMPORTERS AND JOBBERS IN
CROCKERY,
GLASS AND CHINA,
Looking-Glasses,
Britannia and Silver Plated Ware,
Cutlery, &c.
166 RANDOLPH STREET,
CHICAGO, ILL.

☞ Assorted Packages for Country Trade always on hand.

M. B. DERRICK.   SAMUEL SALT.

was supposed to be useless, and t was regarded only as an obstruction to the excavation of the canal. It was discovered a year or two after that fragments of the stone which had been exposed to the air for a few months had become harder. It was, however, with much difficulty that builders were induced to give a trial to what is now regarded as the very best and most elegant building-material in the country. Soft to the chisel, it is hard in the finished wall; and devoid of the glare of white marble, it possesses that hue of the Parthenon which, Dr. Wordsworth says, looks as though it had been "quarried out of the golden light of an Athenian sunset."

THE NICHOLSON PAVEMENT.

As Chicago was the first city to adopt this style of street pavement, it may be proper to give a brief description of it. It is considered far superior and more durable and economical than stone, which is so popular in other cities.

In laying down this pavement, the ground is first levelled or rounded off, so as to conform with the grade, then covered evenly with a coating of sand. Next comes the substructure, which is a flooring of pine boards an inch thick, laid close together in courses lengthwise of the street. The flooring is well tarred on both sides with hot tar and pitch. Upon this substructure the upper stratum of blocks is placed. They are of pine, sawed three inches thick, six inches long, and from six to ten inches wide, and, after being dipped in coal-tar, are set up on end across the street from curb to curb, with their broad faces fronting up and down the street. The first line of blocks being thus set, a line of pickets or strips of board, three inches wide, are placed on edge between the rows, every row being nailed through the picket into the blocks and penetrating the board below, thus making the whole close and tight. Then another row of blocks dipped in hot coal-tar as before is set up against the strip, and so on alternately until completed. There is left between each two consecutive rows of blocks a continuous groove or cell, seven-eighths of an inch wide and three inches deep, extending from curb to curb. The filling of these grooves is the next operation, and this is done with the use of screened gravel and hot coal-tar. The gravel is heated hot and then filled into the cells level with the surface; the coal-tar,

A. H. West

Arthur Farrar

J. J. Crombly

OFFICE OF

WEST, FARRAR & CROMBY

MANUFACTURERS FOR

Wheeler & Wilson Sewing Machines

Chicago, Ill.

106 LAKE STREET

ROYAL BAKING POWDER.

A friend and necessity in every family.

MANUFACTURED AT

209 & 211 Washington St., Chicago.

☞ *For sale by all Grocers.*

AUGUST SCHWARZ'S
BOSTON FANCY STEAM DYE-HOUSE.

158 Illinois St., 2d door west of N. Clark St., Chicago, Ill.

Every description of Silks, Velvets, Woollen Goods, Crape Shawls, etc., colored to any desirable shade, with the finest lustre and finishing. Particular attention given to the cleaning of Silk Dresses, Broche Shawls, etc.; also to the cleaning and re-bleaching of Crape Shawls, Lace Collars, and Lace Curtains. All kinds of Carpets cleaned. Plumes cleaned, dyed, or curled. Kid Gloves cleaned and dyed. Gentlemen's Coats, Pants, and Vests cleaned, dyed, and repaired in the best style. Merchants' Goods dyed.

Branch Offices 107 S. Clark St., & 193 W. Lake St.

R. M. PEARE,

MANUFACTURERS' AGENT & DEALER IN

IRON & WOOD WORKING
MACHINERY.

Northwestern Manufacturers' Supply Depot,

55 SOUTH WELLS St.,
Chicago, Ill.

P. L. GARRITY,

Manufacturing Confectioner,

AND

Jobber in Nuts, Fruits, Fancy Groceries, and Cigars.

39 RANDOLPH ST., CHICAGO

"P. L. G." "GARRITY'S OWN."

CIGARS.

Having exclusive control of the above brands of Cigars, I am prepared to offer special inducements to the Trade.

after being heated, is poured upon the hot gravel until the cells are filled. The composition thus formed is compactly rammed down. The whole surface is then thoroughly covered with hot coal-tar mixed with pitch, and immediately covered with fine gravel and common sand, mixed in about equal proportions, three-quarters of an inch thick. When this is done, the pavement is complete and ready for use.

THE DOUGLAS MONUMENT.

The grave of Illinois' honored son will ever remain an attractive spot. At Cottage Grove, four miles from the Court House, upon a beautiful plateau, is to be found the grave and monument of that illustrious statesman, Stephen Arnold Douglas.

The monument, which is rapidly approaching completion, may be described as follows: A circular platform base, fifty-two feet in diameter, and two and a half feet from the ground; another base, with steps, rising three feet above the circular base, upon which is constructed the sepulchre,—with projecting pedestals, at four corners, eleven feet high, with surrounding walls five feet thick; within is a chamber ten feet square. In the centre of the chamber is a sarcophagus, to be seen by the visitor through an open-work iron door. Upon the sepulchre is a pedestal twenty-two feet high, and a composite column, forty-four in height, rests upon that; a base, resting on the column six feet high, for the reception of a statue of the Senator, twelve feet high, making the height of the entire monument about one hundred feet.

The monument is embellished with many devices and symbolical figures, very beautifully wrought in marble.

The grounds, upon which are the grave and monument, formerly belonged to the Douglas estate, and was purchased from Mrs. Douglas for $30,000. The cost of the monument will be about $80,000.

The place may be reached by the Cottage Grove line of cars, which start from the corner of Lake and State streets.

CHAMBER OF COMMERCE BUILDING

Is situated on the corner of Washington and La Salle streets. It is a handsome structure, ninety-two feet front by one hundred and eighty feet in depth, built of Athens marble, and costing about $400,000 in its erection. The meeting-room, where daily transactions of millions of dollars take place,

ARTISTIC PHOTOGRAPHY.

NORTHWESTERN PHOTOGRAPH GALLERY,

No. 114 S. Clark St.,

CHICAGO, ILL.

S. M. FASSETT, PROPRIETOR.

This Gallery is fitted up in a style of elegance second to none in the country, and furnished with every requisite for the production of first-class work in every variety of style.

The Specimens of Art on exhibition in the parlors attract hundreds of visitors weekly.

The new size CABINET PORTRAITS, a specialty.

☞ *Stereoscopic Illustrations of the City on view and for sale at the Gallery.*

SMITH & DEXTER,

Produce Commission Merchants,

No. 10 Dearborn Street,

CHICAGO, ILL.

We give particular attention to both buying and selling GRAIN, SEEDS, BEEF, PORK, TALLOW, HIDES, WOOL, BROOM-CORN, and DRIED FRUITS.

We have constantly under our personal supervision ample Warehouse room, essential for storing and the successful sale of most kinds of the produce mentioned.

Parties wishing to learn of our character and responsibility, we have permission to refer to —

Hon. I. N. ARNOLD, Chicago.
Messrs. WHITAKER, HARMON & CO., Chicago.
" J. W. DOANE & CO., "
" DAY, ALLEN & CO., "
" GREY, PHELPS & CO., "
" C. H. BECKWITH, Esq., "
THE CITY NATIONAL BANK, "

Office and Warehouse, No. 10 Dearborn Street.

D. W. LAMBERSON & BROTHER,

EXCELSIOR

Silk & Cassimere Hat

Manufacturers,

No. 74 State Street,

D. W. LAMBERSON.
C. V. LAMBERSON.
CHICAGO. *Up-Stairs.*

is on the second floor, a spacious and lofty apartment, one hundred and forty-three feet in length by eighty-seven in width, and forty-five feet in height, decorated with beautiful fresco paintings in the highest style of art. There are about 1500 members, representing all classes of business. The average daily attendance on 'Change is about 1200 members, engaged principally in the flour, grain, lumber, provision, and whisky trade. At about half-past twelve o'clock each day, the Secretary of the Board appears in the gallery and announces the reports of the Eastern markets. The gallery is always open to visitors.

THE COURT HOUSE

Is located in the centre of the square bounded by Clark, Randolph, La Salle, and Washington streets. It is constructed of stone brought from Lockport, New York, and was erected in 1848.

The building is occupied by the various city and county courts, and also by the city government. The basement is used as the County Jail. A splendid view of the city and surrounding country may be obtained from the cupola, to which the visitor has access at any hour of the day. The erection of a City Hall is in contemplation for the exclusive use of the city offices.

UNIVERSITY OF CHICAGO.

Is located at Cottage Grove, about four miles from the Court House. It is built of Athens marble, in the Norman or Romanesque style of architecture. The extreme length of the building is three hundred and thirty-six feet, with a depth of one hundred and seventy-two feet, with wings on the north and south. The height of the main tower is one hundred and fifty-six feet. The north wing is not yet completed. Its external appearance is very much like that of the Smithsonian Institute at Washington, with its lofty towers and minarets.

The University was first opened for instruction in 1858, and then occupied what is now the south wing. The Hon. Stephen A. Douglas was the founder of the institution, and donated the land, ten acres, upon which the structure stands.

The University is always accessible to visitors, and may be reached by the Cottage Grove line of cars from State Street. Another interesting object connected with the University is the

Dearborn Observatory.

Situated west of the main building of the University. It consists of a hollow cone, twenty-seven feet in diameter at the base, and eighty-two feet high, to the floor of the astronomer's room; erected at a cost of twenty-five thousand dollars; and contains the great Alvan Clark telescope, the largest refractor in the world, having an object glass of eighteen and a half inches aperture, and a focal length of twenty-three feet, and weighing six tons.

Visitors are privileged to examine this immense instrument by application to the person in charge.

The Chicago Theological Seminary

Is situated on the west side of Union Park, on the corner of Warren and Reuben streets.

The building is of brick, sixty-five by fifty feet, four stories high, and contains six lecture and reading rooms, and other rooms for about one hundred and fifty students. Cost of building about $100,000.

The institution was established by the Congregational denomination in 1855. It receives, however, students from all denominations. The Seminary may be reached by Madison Street cars.

Presbyterian Theological Seminary.

This institution was founded in 1859 by the Old School branch of the Presbyterian Church. The building, situated on the corner of Fullerton Avenue and Halsted Street, is constructed of pressed brick and stone, five stories high, and presents a very handsome appearance. The Seminary library consists of about seven thousand volumes.

The Young Men's Christian Association,

Now in the twelfth year of its existence, presents a record of prosperity and success scarcely equalled by any similar institution in this country. At the time of its organization it numbered about one hundred and fifty members; at the present time it has enrolled upon its books over two thousand names.

During the last nine years, daily, noon prayer-meetings have been held at its rooms. Its library and reading-room, stocked with religious books, and papers, and periodicals, from all parts of the world, invite the attention of those whose leisure and inclination will permit a visit there. Within the past two years the field of its operations have increased to such an extent that it became

apparent that new quarters must be provided, if the Association should continue its work of usefulness. An appeal was made to the generous Christian public of Chicago to enable the Association to erect a building, the leading object of which should be to accommodate the laborers of the organization. The appeal was nobly responded to. Land was purchased on Madison Street, between Clark and La Salle, and in September, 1867, the largest structure of the kind in the world was dedicated to the interests of the Chicago Young Men's Christian Association.

The main building fronts on Broadway Place, and has a depth of one hundred and twenty feet, with a width of eighty-one feet, four stories high, with a mansard roof. The main entrance to the hall is through the Madison Street front. This room, which has been named Farwell Hall,—in honor of John V. Farwell, the largest contributor to the enterprise,—occupies the whole space within the four walls of the building, and is of the dimensions of one hundred and twenty-one feet by eighty-five feet, and forty-five feet from floor to ceiling. The interior is plainly but neatly finished, and the ceilings are very tastefully frescoed with scriptural subjects. The galleries, of which there are two, extending round three sides of the hall, are so arranged that all the seats have a good view of the speaker's platform. The main floor of the hall is level, with movable chairs. The seats in the gallery are stationary. The entire hall is lighted from the ceiling by double reflectors. This is the largest hall in the West, and capable of comfortably seating three thousand five hundred persons. The ground floor of the building is occupied with stores, while on the second floor are the library, reading-room, lecture-room, and other office rooms for the use of the Association. On the floor above the hall are forty-five dormitories, intended for the use of young men who cannot afford more ample accommodations. The building is painted and grained throughout in imitation of oak and black walnut. The cost of the structure, which is built of marble, was over $200,000.*

Academy of Natural Sciences.

This noble institution, which was organized in 1857, have recently erected a plain, substantial building, entirely fire-proof, upon a lot in the rear of 261 Wabash Avenue. The object of the association is for the increase and diffusion of scientific knowledge, by a Museum, by reading and publication of

* Destroyed by fire, January 7th, 1868.

CHURCH & GOODMAN,

PUBLISHERS,

Booksellers and Stationers,

110 Dearborn Street,

CHICAGO, ILLINOIS.

RELIGIOUS BOOK STORE,

AND

Sabbath-School Depository.

We invite attention to our fine stock of

VALUABLE BOOKS,

which we furnish on the best terms.

CHURCH, GOODMAN & DONNELLEY'S

STEAM BOOK AND JOB

Printing House,

108 & 110 Dearborn Street,

CHICAGO, ILL.

ECONOMICAL
Mutual Life Insurance Company
OF
RHODE ISLAND.

OFFICERS.

SIMON S. BUCKLIN, President.
C. G. McKNIGHT, Vice-President.
WILLIAM Y. POTTER, Secretary.
Hon. ELIZUR WRIGHT, of Mass., Actuary.
A. H. OKIE, M.D., and F. H. PECKHAM, M.D., Medical Examiners.

BOARD OF DIRECTORS.

Maj.-Gen. AMBROSE E. BURNSIDE..Gov. of Rh. Island.
EARL P. MASON..........................Earl P. Mason & Co.
Hon. WILLIAM SPRAGUE........U. S. Senator from R. I.
JOHN CARTER BROWN.........................Brown & Ives.
Hon. LEWIS FAIRBROTHER............North Providence.
SIMON S. BUCKLIN...................................President.
Hon. HENRY B. ANTHONY...... U. S. Senator from R. I.
MOSES B. LOCKWOOD.................A. D. Lockwood & Co.
HENRY HOWARD.............................Coventry, R. I.
A. H. OKIE, M.D.....................................Providence.
ARBA B. DIKE..Providence.
ISAAC H. SOUTHWICK...Pres't American Horse Nail Co.
HORATIO R. NIGHTINGALE......Cornett & Nightingale.
ALEXANDER FARNUM..............Merchant, Providence.
JOSEPH H. BOURN....Bourn & Co., Bankers, Providence.
Hon. JAMES M. PENDLETON................Westerly, R. I.
STEPHEN BROWNELL...Goff, Cranston & Brownell, Prov.
Gen. GEORGE LEWIS COOKE..................Warren, R. I.
ALBERT DAILEY.........Albert Dailey & Co., Providence.
C. G. McKNIGHT, M.D..............................Providence.
JOHN KENDRICK......................................Providence.

Issues all kinds of **POLICIES** at Reduced Rates. Dividends annually in Cash. **PREMIUMS** "Non-Forfeitable" on all the Tab'es.

☞ The Best Protection offered by any Life Company.

W. T. SHUFELDT,
GENERAL WESTERN AGENT,
No. 116½ La Salle Street, (Mercantile Building,)
CHICAGO, ILL.

DOUGLAS MONUMENT
Chicago.

original papers, by a library of works on science, and such other methods as from time to time may be adopted.

The Museum is divided into four cabinets: Zoölogy, Botany, Geology, and Mineralogy. In all there are about fifty thousand specimens. Open to visitors from 10 A. M. till 5 P. M

The Chicago Historical Society,

Which has been organized about twelve, years, have recently erected a noble building on Ontario Street, between North Clark and Dearborn streets. It is an elegant fire-proof structure, built of brick and stone, forty-two feet front, ninety feet in depth, and three stories high; forming only one wing of the main building, which, it is presumed, will be needed before many years. The object of the organization is to prosecute historical collections for the State of Illinois and the Northwest, and for the foundation of a public library of a comprehensive character. Its collections, thus far amounting to about 90,000, consist of rare and valuable books and pamphlets pertaining to the history and antiquities of the country. Also medals, coins, maps, &c.

Its rooms are open every day, Sunday

excepted, for members; and its library privileges to strangers and visitors from 10 o'clock A. M. to 4 o'clock P. M.

The Soldiers' Home.

This noble enterprise, founded in 1863, is located at Cottage Grove, about four miles from the city. It is built of brick, four stories high, and is very admirably arranged throughout for the comfort and convenience of its occupants. The cost of the building was about $47,000. The value of the Home, together with the land upon which it stands, is now estimated at $100,000.

This worthy institution is maintained by private and public contributions, together with a fund realized from the great Northwestern Fair, and gives a home and shelter to all honorably discharged Illinois soldiers or sailors who are unable, by reason of wounds or other disability, to support themselves. The average number of inmates is about one hundred. The building will accommodate nearly two hundred. Visitors always welcome.

Cottage Grove cars from State Street run to the Home.

W. H. C. MILLER & Co.,

Importers & Manufacturers of

Fine Jewelry

AND

DIAMOND WORK,

English, AMERICAN, & Swiss

WATCHES,

Fine Silver & Plated Ware, Table Cutlery, Clocks, Spectacles, etc.

Smith & Nixon's Building, Southwest cor. Washington,

108 & 110 Clark St., Chicago.

W. H. C. Miller & Co. are an old established House, and manufacture their own goods, and sell at WHOLESALE PRICES.

ILLINOIS CENTRAL R. R.,

FOR

PEORIA, SPRINGFIELD, ST. LOUIS, KANSAS CITY, LEAVENWORTH, ST. JOSEPH,

And all parts of the Southwest.

The Shortest, Quickest, and only Direct Route to

CAIRO, MEMPHIS, VICKSBURG, NEW ORLEANS, MOBILE,

And all parts of the South.

---

150 Miles Shorter and 24 Hours Quicker to MEMPHIS and ALL SOUTHERN CITIES, than any other Route.

EXPRESS TRAINS LEAVE CHICAGO DAILY
(Morning and Evening,)

From the Great Central Depot, foot of Lake St.

Only One Change of Cars from Chicago to Memphis, New Orleans, or Mobile.

ELEGANT SLEEPING CARS ON ALL NIGHT TRAINS.

For Through Tickets and Baggage Checks, apply at the Great Central Depot.

M. HUGHITT, Gen'l Sup't.
W. P. JOHNSON, Gen'l Passenger Ag't.

Home for the Friendless.

This noble charity is located at 911 Wabash Avenue. The average number of inmates is about one hundred. Since its establishment in 1858, it has received and provided with homes in city and country, about two thousand women and children. Poor women, as well as children, are given a temporary home until they can find employment. In our visit to the institution, we were much gratified with the general appearance of the entire establishment. It is a model in point of cleanliness, order, judicious management, and practical benevolence

The institution is sustained entirely by voluntary contributions, and we would commend it to the consideration of the benevolent. Visitors kindly welcome at any time.

The Washingtonian Home

Was incorporated in 1867. It occupies a large three-story frame structure, No. 568 to 572 Madison Street, near Union Park. It has accommodations for about sixty persons, and is maintained principally by private contributions, although a small charge is made to those who are able to pay. It is a reformatory establishment for unfortunate inebriates, hundreds of whom can testify to its benefits. Through its kindly influence, many fathers, or husbands, or sons, have been restored to their families, and caused multitudes to rejoice.

Madison-Street cars pass the Home.

The Magdalen Asylum.

Chicago, like every other large city, has its class of outcasts from society, who must be rescued and reformed, or must inevitably infect the moral atmosphere with the taint of vice, and prepare a never-failing supply of inmates for its prisons, hospitals, and almshouses. The above-named institution has been established for the reclamation of the fallen women, with which this city so fearfully abounds. It was founded in 1858, and is under the care and management of the Sisters of the Good Shepherd.

The Asylum is located on the corner of North Market and Hill streets, in the North Division of the city. Visitors not admitted.

The Erring Woman's Refuge.

This praiseworthy institution is situated on Indiana Avenue, corner of Thirty-first Street. The above-named Refuge is intended as a home, not as a place of confinement,—a home where may be found kind looks, affectionate words, earnest entreaty, and wholesome advice,— a home, whose inmates, sheltered by good influences, and withdrawn entirely from the whirlpool of dissipation, may carry out their feeble resolves, to forsake, with Divine assistance, the allurements of sin, and prove by their future lives the sincerity of their efforts. The Refuge was purchased for $10,500. It is a neat commodious building, surrounded with trees, and is capable of sheltering about forty persons. Visitors not admitted, except for the purpose of imparting religious counsel and instruction to its inmates.

Old Ladies' Home.

The object of this Institution is to provide a home for indigent old ladies over sixty years of age. One hundred dollars is charged as an entrance fee; then they are provided for during life without any additional expense. The Home, a three-story frame building, is located on Indiana Avenue, between Twenty-sixth and Twenty-seventh streets. In this establishment many old ladies find a home, who otherwise would have to look to the cold world for support.

Visitors admitted at any time.

The Chicago Orphan Asylum

Was incorporated in 1849 and organized in 1853, its object being to take in, care for, and provide homes for poor orphan children, and recently an additional feature has been added to its objects, namely: to care for the children of deceased Union soldiers.

This Institution has a large four-story brick building for the accommodation of its inmates. Its capacity is sufficient for between four and five hundred children. The Asylum is located on Michigan Avenue, between Twenty-second and Twenty-third streets, on a lot two hundred by three hundred feet in extent, tastefully ornamented with trees, shrubbery, &c., and having a children's playground.

The Asylum is ably sustained by the contributions and yearly subscriptions of the benevolent and charitable people of Chicago, through whose noble liberality it was established, and thus far successfully maintained. The amount of good that has been accomplished by this institution to unfortunate, friendless, and homeless children, cannot be estimated. Hundreds of little ones have been rescued from wretchedness, kindly cared for, and when arriving at a proper age, provided with good homes. Every sentiment

ESTABLISHED 1847.

NUMSEN, CARROLL & CO.,
18 Light Street,
BALTIMORE.

BRANCH HOUSE,
39 State Street,
Chicago.

PACKERS OF
Canned Oysters,
FRUITS, VEGETABLES, JELLIES,
PICKLES, PRESERVES, ETC.

Sole Agent for the

A. Field Oysters,
39 State St., Chicago.

E. F. SLOCUM,
WHOLESALE DEALER IN
Table Glass Ware,
CUTLERY,
Lamps, Chandeliers, &c
122 CLARK STREET,
CHICAGO.

"THE PRESS."
The Leading Daily Newspaper in Pennsylvania.
EXTENSIVE IMPROVEMENTS!
GREAT INDUCEMENTS!

THE DAILY PRESS
CONTAINS THE LATEST INTELLIGENCE FROM ALL PARTS OF THE WORLD. Besides special telegrams, *it has all the dispatches of the Associated Press from every part of the United States and from all parts of Europe.*

Terms of Subscription.
One copy, one year, $8.00; six months, $4.00; three months, $2.00. *Payment required invariably in advance.*

THE WEEKLY PRESS
CONTAINS A COMPLETE COMPENDIUM OF THE NEWS OF THE WEEK, and all the leading editorials from the Daily, besides a large amount of interesting matter prepared expressly for the weekly issue. It will be in all respects A FIRST-CLASS FAMILY JOURNAL.

Terms of Subscription.
One copy, one year, $2.00; five copies, one year, $9.00; ten copies, one year, $17.50; twenty copies, one year, $33.00. To clubs, *where the papers are sent to one address,* the following reduction will be made: five copies, one year, $8.50; ten copies, one year, $16.50; twenty copies, one year, $30.00. A copy will be furnished *gratis* for each club of ten, or more, to one address, for one year. *Payment required invariably in advance.*

TRI-WEEKLY PRESS.
TERMS.—$4.00 per annum; $2.00 for six months; $1.00 for three months.   Address   JOHN W. FORNEY,
Editor and Publisher,
Philadelphia, Pa

of humanity appeals to the public to foster and amply support an institution that is so beneficent in its purpose. Visitors are admitted from 10 A. M. to 5 P. M.

The Half Orphan Asylum

Occupies a spacious building well arranged for the purpose to which it is adapted, on the corner of Wells and Wisconsin streets. It is under the management of ladies of various religious denominations. A large number of the children are those whose fathers fell in the recent war. The benevolence of the Christian appears truly in a work like this. What friend of his country, of humanity, does not wish well to such a noble institution! Strangers admitted from 10 o'clock A. M. to 4 P. M.

The Catholic Asylum for Boys

Is under the care of the Christian Brothers. It is the legal guardian of all children who may be committed to it by the voluntary act of parents or by the order of a police magistrate. The children are taught various trades, and instructed in all the branches of a common-school education.

Roman Catholic Orphan Asylums.

These Asylums are located at 265 and 267 Wabash Avenue. The St. Joseph's Asylum for boys, and the St. Mary's for girls, are both under the care of the Sisters of Mercy.

The Reform School.

The objects of the institution are, to rescue from the ills and the temptations of poverty and neglect those who have been left without a parent's care; to reclaim from moral exposure those who are treading the paths of danger; and to offer to those whose only training would otherwise have been in the walks of vice, if not of crime, the blessings of education and industry.

The school is under the management of a Board of Guardians selected by the Common Council. It is situated about six miles from the city, on the road to Hyde Park. Belonging to the institution are about forty acres of land, which is kept under cultivation by the boys in the school. The institution may be reached by the Illinois Central Railroad.

Chicago Eye and Ear Infirmary.

This commodious hospital is located on Pearson Street west of State. It is open for

the gratuitous treatment of the poor who are afflicted with diseases of the eye and ear. Persons applying for gratuitous admission are expected to bring satisfactory evidence of respectable character and indigent circumstances. Pay patients are also admitted, and the managers are thus enabled to diffuse its advantages more widely among the poor than they otherwise could do.

State Street cars lead to the Institution.

THE RUSH MEDICAL COLLEGE

Was founded in 1837. The present building was erected in 1867, at a cost of $75,000. It stands on the corner of North Dearborn and Indiana streets, fronting on the latter. It is built of brick with stone dressings, sixty feet front and seventy-two feet in depth, four stories high, and has fine accommodations for about seven hundred students. The lecture-rooms are commodious, and that part appropriated to dissection is admirably adapted to the purpose, being large, well ventilated, and supplied with all the conveniences necessary for the comfort of those engaged in the study of Practical Anatomy.

The Museum contains ample materials for

study, in wax models, anatomical preparations, morbid and healthy specimens, both dry and wet, and a large collection of anatomical, surgical, and obstetrical plates, of the size of life. A cabinet of minerals, specimens of the materia medica, and philosophical instruments, &c. The Museum is accessible to visitors.

CHICAGO MEDICAL COLLEGE.

This institution was founded in 1858, and is now in a very prosperous condition. For nine years past this has been the only Medical College in the United States whose curriculum embraced the whole series of Medical Sciences, a full corps of thirteen Professorships, a long College Term, and a successive order of study, with Hospital Clinical instruction, as an essential part of the Senior course, and one of the conditions for graduation.

The College building, located at 1015 State Street above Twenty-second Street, is a plain brick structure, and contains a lecture-room, museum, dissecting room, laboratory, professors' and students' rooms, &c. The Museum, considering its age, is amply supplied. We would recommend our readers to avail them-

DIAMONDS,
WATCHES,
JEWELRY,
AND
CLOCKS.

We have spared no pains to keep, and introduce into this market, the VERY BEST class of Watches, and our connection with the Geneva and New York Houses enables us to sell them in most elegant cases, (of our own workmanship,) as low as a cheaper class of Watches have usually been sold here.

Solid Gold Jewelry, Full Pearl Bridal Sets,

Diamond, Emerald, Hyacinth, Sapphire, and Mosaic, full and half sets; Bracelets, Finger and Handkerchief Rings, &c., &c.

ELEGANT SILVER AND SILVER-PLATED GOODS.

Exclusive Manufacturers of the superb Tiffany styles of

MASKED AND GRECIAN SPOONS AND FORKS.

GORHAM & CO.'S NORTHWESTERN SILVER WARE CO'S GOODS.

Richly-Chased Tea and Tete-a-Tete Sets, Cups, Goblets, Urns, Ladles, Napkin Rings, &c.; Preserve, Jelly, Ice-Cream, and Sugar Spoons, Knives, Forks, &c.

A very large assortment of

CLOCKS,

OF OUR OWN MANUFACTURE, CONSTANTLY ON HAND.

GILES, BRO. & CO.,

142 . . . . LAKE STREET. 142

CHICAGO, ILL.

DANIEL BARCLAY,

141 State Street,

CHICAGO.

LYMAN BRIDGES,
DEALER IN
BUILDING MATERIALS
AND
READY-MADE HOUSES,
70 WASHINGTON STREET (Cor. Dearborn),

CHICAGO, ILL.

Warehouses: 226 to 246 Carroll Street. 85 to 101 Morgan Street. 84 to 98 Sangamon Street. Connecting with all Railways in the City.

HEIMERDINGER & CO.,
GREAT WESTERN
Boot and Shoe Emporium,
115 South Clark Street,

(Methodist Church Block,)

CHICAGO.

selves of the opportunity to examine this Museum.

Open to visitors during the sessions—from October to March.

State Street cars pass the College.

Cook County Hospital

Occupies a brick building on Arnold Street between Eighteenth and Nineteenth Streets. It was erected in 1856 by the city at a cost of $75,000. A four-story brick structure, capable of accommodating about three hundred patients.

St. Luke's Hospital,

Situated at 669 State Street, was founded in 1864, and is under the control of the Episcopal denomination. It is open, however, to persons of any color, creed, or country. It has accommodation for about one hundred patients.

Mercy Hospital.

This Institution, under the charge of the religious order of the Sisters of Mercy, is situated on Calumet Avenue between Twenty-fifth and Twenty-sixth streets. The accommodation for patients, which is limited, is excellent in every respect. It is a receptacle in cases of sudden accidents. It is not altogether gratuitous; but to such as are able to pay, it offers most important advantages.

Lake Hospital.

A spacious structure, consisting of a main building two stories in height, with two wings, one story each, built of wood, and cost about $14,000. Located on the corner of North State Street and North Avenue. This is not an asylum for the support of the destitute, but an hospital for their cure when sick. A limited number of pay patients are received, which is but an extension of its charity; for whatever profits are derived from this source, go to increase the ability of the institution to relieve the poor.

The Jewish Hospital

Is situated on North La Salle Street between Goethe and Schiller streets. It is built of red brick, eighty feet by forty, two and a half stories high, and costs about $40,000.

The building, although it presents a handsome exterior, is constructed with an eye to durability and comfort. Corner-stone laid September 2, 1867.

Union Mutual Life Ins. Co.

ASSETS OVER $3,000,000.
☞ Annual Dividends to the Insured. ☜

BABCOCK, CLARK & Co.,
GENERAL AGENTS FOR ILLINOIS AND IOWA.

OFFICES:
Northwest corner of Brady and Second Streets, Davenport, Iowa.
128 LA SALLE STREET, CHICAGO, ILL.

F. BABCOCK.   D. D. BABCOCK.   L. C. CLARK.

MERRILL & HOPKINS,
AGENTS FOR THE MANUFACTURERS OF

Queensware, Glassware,

SILVER-PLATED WARE, BRITANNIA WARE,
ROCK & YELLOW WARE, Etc. Etc.
Assorted and Original Packages constantly on hand.

Office, 20 Lake St., Chicago, Ill.

H. C. CHAMPION & Co.,
COMMISSION MERCHANTS,

JOBBERS IN

FOREIGN AND DOMESTIC FRUITS,
FANCY GROCERIES,
Factory, Hamburg, and Western Reserve

CHEESE,

OYSTERS, FIRE WORKS, Etc.

No. 9 Clark St., Chicago.

CHAS. LEEDS & Co.,

GENERAL

COMMISSION & FORWARDING MERCHANTS,

DEALERS IN

FLOUR, GRAIN, & PRODUCE.

—ALSO—

HARD WOOD, LUMBER, & COOPERAGE.

160 South Water St.,
CHICAGO, Ill.

TURKISH & ELECTRO-THERMAL BATHS,
WITH
MEDICAL MANIPULATION & HYGIENIC TREATMENT.

All Diseases that are curable are cured. DRUGS are NOT used. City References given.

Advice by mail for home treatment, $10.

Rooms, 5, 7, and 9 Major Block,
corner La Salle & Madison Sts.,
CHICAGO, Ill.

JOHN WINGRAVE,
Hygienic Physician.

Dispensaries.

CHICAGO CITY DISPENSARY, State St. near 22d St.
CHARITY DISPENSARY, Rush Medical College.
HAHNEMANN DISPENSARY, 168 South Clark Street.
EYE AND EAR DISPENSARY, 16 East Pearson Street.

LIBRARIES AND READING-ROOMS.

Historical Society Library.

Situated on Ontario Street between North Clark and Dearborn. Contains about eight thousand volumes and sixty thousand pamphlets, together with many interesting and valuable maps, coins, charts, &c. Open from 10 A. M. to 4 P. M.

Young Men's Library.

This is the oldest and largest regular library in the city,—established in 1841,—and contains twenty thousand volumes. They have recently received a very valuable contribution from the English Government, a complete set of the Patent Reports of the English Government from the beginning, numbering about two thousand five hundred volumes, about the size of Webster's Unabridged Dictionary. There are but four sets of this collection in the United States: one in the Patent Office, one in the Astor Library, one in New York State Library at Albany, one in Boston Public Library. This one here is the only one in the Northwest. The Library is located in Library Hall Building, corner of La Salle and Randolph streets. Open from 9 A. M. to 10 P. M.

The Chicago Law Library

Numbers about five thousand volumes. Rooms at the Law Institute in the Court House. Open daily.

Christian Association Library.

The Library belonging to this Association is not very large, numbering only about seven thousand volumes, mostly of a religious character. The reading-room connected with it is well supplied with the papers and periodicals of this and foreign countries. Rooms in the Association building, No. 148 Madison Street. All are welcome. Open from 9 A. M. till 10 P. M. of each week-day.

SOCIETIES.

AMERICAN BAPTIST HOME MISS., 51 La Salle Street.
AMERICAN MISSIONARY UNION, 51 La Salle Street.
AMER. BOARD OF COMMISSIONERS, 51 La Salle Street.

A GUIDE TO CHICAGO.

AMERICAN HOME MISS. SOCIETY, 51 La Salle Street.
AMERICAN MISSIONARY ASSOCIATION, Lombard Block.
AMER. SUNDAY SCHOOL UNION, 109 Dearborn Street.
AMERICAN TRACT SOCIETY, 7 Custom House Place.
AMER. TRACT SOCIETY (Boston), 51 La Salle Street.
AUDUBON CLUB, 77 Dearborn Street.
BIBLE SOCIETY, 170 Clark Street.
BOHEMIAN CLUB, McVickers' Theatre Building.
CALEDONIAN CLUB, 101 Washington Street.
CHICAGO HISTORICAL SOCIETY, Ontario near Clark St.
CHESS CLUB, Dearborn and Washington Streets.
FREEDMEN'S ASSOCIATION, 109 Monroe Street.
HEBREW RELIEF ASSOCIATION, Metropolitan Build'g.
IMMIGRANT AID SOCIETY, 97 Kinzie Street.
IRVING LITERARY ASSOCIATION, Morrison's Block.
MENDELSSOHN SOCIETY, 81 Wabash Avenue.
MUSICAL UNION, Clark and Washington Streets.
MERCANTILE ASSOCIATION, 36 Dearborn Street.
ST. GEORGE'S SOCIETY, 226 Clark Street.
SVEA SOCIETY, 111 Kinzie Street.
SONS OF ERIN, 82 Randolph Street.
TOTAL ABSTINENCE SOCIETY, 78 Dearborn Street.
YOUNG MEN'S CHRISTIAN ASSOC., 148 Madison St.

PUBLIC SCHOOLS.

The public schools of the city are among the very best in the United States. The buildings are large, handsome, and convenient; much care is taken with regard to the ventilation of the rooms and the exercise of the pupils; the salaries of the teachers range from four hundred to twenty-four hundred dollars a year. In the High School, as well as in the common schools, colored children mingle with the other pupils. No little child is allowed to pass more than half an hour without exercise. In the higher classes, the physical exercises occur about once an hour; the windows are thrown open, the pupils rise, and all the class imitate the motions of the teacher for five minutes. The boys in the High School have a lesson daily in out-door gymnastics. The girls have a variety of exercises which combine work and play in an agreeable manner. Thus it will be observed the parents of Chicago are not unmindful of the physical as well as mental training of their children.

Twenty-eight years ago there was not a single school-house in the city; at present there are some twenty-five, with over forty thousand children instructed therein.

PUBLIC PARKS.

Although Chicago is a city of a quarter of a million inhabitants, it is not so compactly built as to need parks, as breathing

EMPIRE
Shuttle Sewing Machine.

Received the *first* premium as the best *Family* and *Manufacturing Machine* at the Grand Exhibition of the American Institute, October 26th, 1867: it being subjected to the severest tests by sewing-machine experts, in competition with all the first-class machines.

It has a straight needle, perpendicular action, makes the *Lock* or *Shuttle Stitch*, which will *neither rip nor ravel*, and is alike on both sides. It is the MOST NOISELESS of all the shuttle machines.

It Hems, Fells, Binds, Braids, Tucks, Quilts, Plaits, and *Gathers*. Either as a *Family* or *Manufacturing Machine* it has **NO SUPERIOR**.

Machine Silks, Thread, Needles, and Oil, finest qualities, and at lowest market prices, wholesale and retail.

HILDER & THOMPSON.
General Agents for the Northwest,
161 LAKE St., CHICAGO.

J. WRIGHT'S RESTAURANT,

65 Washington Street,

(Crosby's Opera House,)

CHICAGO, ILL.,

Is decidedly the best appointed, finest, most extensive and stylish place of the kind in the city. He always buys the best in the market, and has it cooked and served in a style that cannot fail to please the most fastidious.

WEDDINGS,
Public and Private Parties,

Supplied on reasonable terms, at short notice.

HIS BRANCH DINING-ROOM
AT THE MICHIGAN SOUTHERN DEPOT

is unsurpassed by any place of the kind in the United States.

CROSBY'S OPERA HOUSE.
Chicago.

JOHN B. WIGGINS,
FASHIONABLE
CARD ENGRAVER.
Wedding, Visiting, and Invitation
CARDS
OF THE LATEST STYLES
NOTARIAL, LODGE, AND BANKERS' SEALS

Manufacturer of the Celebrated

White Metal Door-Plates, Church, Hotel, and House Numbers, Door-Knobs, Blind and Sash-Fastenings, &c., &c.

No. 6 SOUTH CLARK STREET
CHICAGO.

New School Desks, with Folding Seats.

Patented, September 10, 1867.
HENRY M. SHERWOOD,
Manufacturer and Dealer in
GENERAL SCHOOL MERCHANDISE,

Has the latest and most desirable styles, and **Best School Desks and Seats** to be found in the Northwest. Castings sold separately if desired. SHERWOOD'S PATENT INK-WELL FOR SCHOOLS, OUTLINE MAPS, GLOBES, SCHOOL APPARATUS, LIQUID SLATING FOR BLACKBOARDS, &c., &c.

☞ Send for Illustrated Catalogue and Price List.

HENRY M. SHERWOOD, 107 Monroe St.,
First Door West of the Post-Office.   CHICAGO, ILL.

L. M. PRENTISS & CO.,
WHOLESALE DEALERS IN

Beef, Pork, Lard, Hams,
AND ALL
SMOKED MEATS.
AND
COMMISSION MERCHANTS,
152 SOUTH WATER STREET,
CHICAGO.

BRYANT & STRATTON'S
Commercial College,
CORNER OF
Clark and Washington Streets,

Chicago, Ill.

places, like many Eastern cities; yet we are happy to witness the opening and ornamenting of these public places, for we regard them among the most beautiful and salutary of our public improvements.

Dearborn Park.

Upon this spot was situated the Sanitary Fair Building in 1865. The Park contains about one and a half acres, and is enclosed with an iron railing. It occupies the space bounded by Randolph and Washington streets, and Michigan Avenue and Dearborn Place. It formerly belonged to the General Government, and was ceded to the city to be used exclusively as a public park.

Lincoln Park

Is located near the city cemetery, commanding a beautiful view of the lake. It contains some sixty acres, with a variety of fine trees, handsome walks and carriage-ways, and will in time possess all the essentials of a picturesque park—pond, stream, hill, rock, plain, and slope. The attractions are greater than that of any other, and it may properly be called *the* park of Chicago.

Lake Park,

So called,' will in time be worthy of the above name. The Board of Public Works have decided to fill up what is now the Basin, on the east side of Michigan Avenue, and ornament it with trees, shrubbery, flowers, and fountains, rendering it the finest promenade in the city.

Union Park

Is situated in the West Division and contains sixteen acres. It is bounded on the north by Lake Street, south by Warren, west by Reuben Street, and on the east by Byron Place. It is only partially improved, the design being to ornament it with artificial hills, rocks, and ponds. This Park is located in the vicinity of what may be termed the *West End* of Chicago.

Jefferson Park

Is a smaller one, situated only two blocks south of Union Park. It contains about five acres, covering one square.

Vernon Park

Lies about half a mile south of Union Park, on Polk Street. It is scarcely worthy the name of a park, being so small.

THE MERCHANTS, FARMERS & MECHANICS' SAVINGS BANK

S.H. FLEETWOOD, PREST.

13 CLARK ST.

(INCORPORATED.)

$5.00 per Week.

A Deposit of Five Dollars each Week will with the Interest allowed by this Bank produce the following results:

In Five Years	$1,503.50
In Ten Years	3,324.25
In Fifteen Years	6,339.80
In Twenty Years	9,819.20
In Twenty Five Years	14,793.70
In Thirty Years	21,385.05

Amount deposited in Thirty Years $7,800.00
Amount of Interest on same 13,585.05
21,385.05

The Business of this Institution is confined exclusively to the Care of Savings Deposits and Trust Funds.
No general or Commercial Banking Business is transacted.

SYDNEY MYERS, CASHR.

CHICAGO, FEB. 22d 1861.

Interest at rate of SIX PER CENT per annum, is paid on Sums of Five Dollars and upwards.
Married Women & Minors may deposit in their own names for their own use.
Office Hours from 10 A.M. to 3 P.M.
Also from 6 P.M. to 8 P.M. Saturdays.

Washington Park

Contains about three acres, with but little ornamentation or anything to make it attractive. It occupies the square bounded by Chestnut, Clark, and Dearborn streets.

PLACES OF ENTERTAINMENT.

The Crosby Opera House,

Which gained so much notoriety in connection with the "Great Gift Enterprise," is located on Washington Street, between State and Dearborn. It has a front of one hundred and forty feet, with a depth of one hundred and seventy-nine feet, and four stories high, with an extensive mansard roof. It is built of Athens marble, somewhat in the Corinthian style of architecture. It is said to be the largest and most elegant edifice of the kind on this continent. The auditorium, which is approached by a broad and spacious stairway, is eighty-six feet wide, one hundred and fifty-five feet in depth, and sixty feet from floor to ceiling; it is scarcely equalled in its decorations and arrangements, and is divided into five parts,—the orchestra circle, the parquet, the parquet circle, the dress circle or first gallery, the second or family circle,—all of which is fitted up in magnificent style.

The entire cost of this splendid building was about $500,000. It was completed and opened to the public in May, 1865.

McVicker's Theatre.

This spacious edifice stands on Madison Street, between State and Dearborn. It was erected at a cost of about $80,000, and is capable of accommodating 2000 people. The interior is admirably arranged, and the seats, which are easy and comfortable, give a fine view of the immense stage, which is eighty feet deep and forty-eight feet wide. This Theatre is usually successful in its entertainments.

Col. Wood's Museum

Is located on Randolph Street, between Clark and Dearborn. It contains several large halls filled with a variety of curiosities; besides numerous paintings and statuary, an extensive mineralogical and ornithological collection, together with other objects of interest and wonder.

Dramatic entertainments are given in the Lecture Room every evening by a stock company.

STATE STREET LAUNDRY,
215 STATE STREET,
CHICAGO.

The Quickest, Cheapest, and Best.

LADIES' LINEN Fluted and Finished equal to any in the City.

PARCELS called for and delivered free of charge.

Orders by Post promptly attended to.

Wholesale and Retail
BUILDERS' HARDWARE.

Nails,

Weights, and

Cord

Brushes,

Twines,

Wringers,

Stoves,

Cutlery,

Wooden Ware,

Filters,

Dumb-Bells,

Baskets,

WATER-COOLERS AND REFRIGERATORS.

Our stock of Light, Fancy, and Housekeeping Hardware is very large.

We are Sole Agents for the EAGLE GAS COOKING AND HEATING STOVES.

Plain TIN WARE, TOILET WARE, LANTERNS, &c.

T. B. & H. M. SEAVEY,
82 Randolph Street,
CHICAGO.

A. RANNEY,
RECTIFIER AND WHOLESALE DEALER IN
WINES
AND
FOREIGN AND DOMESTIC LIQUORS,
Manufacturer of the celebrated Copper Distilled
"Mount Vernon Whiskey."
MOUNT VERNON BITTERS, &c.
185 KINZIE STREET,
(Revere House Block,)
CHICAGO, ILL.

N. B.—Persons wishing anything in the Liquor line, either in City or Country, can always depend on getting what they order, promptly, and of the best quality, for the money paid. Liberal terms of payment will be given to responsible parties.

A. RANNEY.

THE
EXCELSIOR LIFE INSURANCE COMPANY
OF
NEW YORK.

Its *perfect organization ensures security and profit* to policy holders. *Faithfulness* to the *Trust* imposed characterizes its management. It is *equal* to any and *excelled* by none.

GEORGE FARR,
General Agent,
Major Block, corner Madison and La Salle Sts.
CHICAGO

German Theatre.

The above theatre, patronized chiefly by our German fellow-citizens, is situated on North Wells Street, corner of Indiana. The performances are given exclusively in the German language.

Arlington Hall.

This is about the only place in the city where burnt cork performances are given. It is a good place to "while away an hour." Situated on Washington Street, between Dearborn and Clark, opposite the Court House.

Public Halls.

ARLINGTON HALL, Washington Street, near Clark.
APOLLO HALL, Lake and South Water Streets.
AURORA HALL, Milwaukee and Second Streets.
BRYAN HALL, Clark Street.
BLANEY HALL, Randolph and La Salle Streets.
BURLINGTON HALL, State and Seventeenth Streets.
CITY HALL, Court House.
CROSBY MUSIC HALL, 88 State Street.
DEMOCRATIC HALL, Clark and Monroe Streets.
DRUIDS HALL, South Water, near Wells Street.
FARWELL HALL, Young Men's Ch. A. Building.
FENIAN HALL, Randolph and Wells Streets.
GERMAN TURN HALL, Clark and Chicago Avenue.
HARMONY HALL, 48 Clark Street.
HORNER'S HALL, 82 West Randolph Street.

JACKSON HALL, 55 La Salle Street.
KINZIE HALL, Kinzie, near Clark Street.
LIBRARY HALL, Randolph and La Salle Streets.
LIGHT GUARD HALL, State and Randolph Streets.
LINCOLN HALL, Lake and Franklin Streets.
MASONIC HALL, Dearborn, near Washington Streets.
MASONIC HALL, La Salle, near Madison Street.
METROPOLITAN HALL, Randolph and La Salle Sts.
NIPPE'S HALL, Vedder and Pleasant Streets.
ODD FELLOWS' HALL, 48 Clark Street.
PEOPLE'S HALL, Taylor and Morgan Streets.
ST. GEORGE'S HALL, 226 Clark Street.
SMITH & NIXON'S HALL, Washington and Clark Sts.
TEUTONIA HALL, 235 Randolph Street.
WARNER'S HALL, 124 Randolph Street.
WORKINGMEN'S HALL, Twelfth and Walter Streets.
WITKOWSKY, Clark and Monroe Streets.

POST-OFFICE.

This elegant and imposing building, situated on the corner of Dearborn and Monroe streets, was erected by the General Government in 1859. It is constructed of marble and iron, and is probably one of the most expensive public buildings in the city.

The building was erected by the Government as a Custom House, and the upper portions of it are occupied as such in connection with the United States Courts,

Offices of Internal Revenue, and United States Marshal.

The Post-Office is open during the following hours: from April 1st to November 1st, 7 A. M. till 7½ P. M.; from November 1st to April 1st, 8 A. M. till 7½ P. M.; on Sundays, from 8.30 A. M. till 10.15 A. M.

A large number of street letter-boxes are stationed throughout the city, from which collections are made five times daily.

FIRE DEPARTMENT.

This most efficient department consists of twelve Steamers, two Hand-Engines, two Hook-and-Ladder Trucks, and thirteen Hose Carts, operated by about three hundred men, half the number of whom are paid, and half volunteers. There are one hundred and seventy-one fire-alarm boxes in various parts of the city, each connected by telegraph with the central office, in the tower of the Court House. The Commissioner's and Fire Marshal's offices are at 140 Madison Street, in the Young Men's Christian Association Building.

POLICE DEPARTMENT.

The Police are under the control of three Commissioners elected by the people, and a Superintendent and Deputy appointed by said Commissioners. The Headquarters, or Central Station, is located at 140 Madison Street. Two hundred and fifty men compose the entire force. The following are the stations:

CITY ARMORY, corner Franklin and Adams Streets.
FIRST PRECINCT, corner Archer and 22d Streets.
SECOND PRECINCT, 14 North Union Street.
SUB STATION, corner West Lake and Paulina Streets.
THIRD PRECINCT, Michigan Av., near Dearborn St.
SUB STATION, cor. North Avenue and Larrabee St.

BOARDS.

BOARD OF PUBLIC WORKS, 17 Wells Street.
BOARD OF HEALTH, 140 Madison Street.
BOARD OF POLICE COMMISSIONERS, 140 Madison St.
BOARD OF FIRE COMMISSIONERS, 140 Madison Street.

BANKS.

The Banks of Chicago may with propriety be numbered among the public buildings,

TYLER, ULLMANN & CO.,
Bankers and Dealers
IN
GOVERNMENT SECURITIES,
GOLD, STOCKS,
GOLD DUST,
AND
Local Securities.

We are members of the "NEW YORK STOCK EXCHANGE" and GOLD BOARD, and all orders for STOCKS and GOLD executed with promptness and dispatch.

Office, cor. Lake & Dearborn Sts.
CHICAGO.

Agricultural College Scrip and Land Warrants a Specialty.

TYLER, WRENN & CO.,
18 Wall Street,
NEW YORK CITY.

Seals, Stencils, Door Plates, Wedding & Visiting Cards.

Wood Engraving, Lithographing, Manufacturer of Seal Presses.

A. MARKS,
GENERAL ENGRAVER,
47 Clark Street, Chicago.

E. BALL & Co.,
MANUFACTURERS OF

THE
WORLD'S MOWER & REAPER,
OHIO REAPER & MOWER,
AND
TORNADO THRESHER.
Canton, Ohio.

Western Office, 186 & 188 Washington St.,
CHICAGO.

and, taken as a whole, are certainly very beautiful as specimens of architecture.

There are sixteen National Banks, with a capital of over $6,000,000, located as follows:

FIRST NATIONAL, S. W. corner Lake and Clark Sts.
SECOND NATIONAL, N. W. corner Lake and Clark Sts.
THIRD NATIONAL, corner Dearborn and Randolph.
FOURTH NATIONAL, cor. Monroe & Custom House Pl
FIFTH NATIONAL. 50 La Salle Street.
COMMERCIAL, 55 Dearborn Street.
MANUFACTURERS', 154 Lake Street.
MECHANICS', 156 Lake Street.
MERCHANTS', 36 Clark Street.
NORTH WESTERN, Chamber Commerce Building.
CITY, Chamber Commerce Building.
TRADERS', 40 South Clark Street.
UNION, corner Lake and La Salle Streets.
TREASURY, 66 Washington Street.
MARINE, Lake and La Salle Streets.
BANK OF MONTREAL, 48 La Salle Street.

Savings Banks.

The first Savings Bank in Chicago was established in 1857: since then the following have been organized:

MERCHANTS' SAVINGS LOAN AND TRUST COMPANY,
        corner Lake and Dearborn Streets
MERCHANTS', FARMERS', AND MECHANICS',
        13 Clark Street.
STATE SAVINGS INSTITUTION, 82 La Salle Street.

TELEGRAPH OFFICES.

WESTERN UNION, S. E. cor. of Lake and Clark Sts.

TELEGRAPH COLLEGES.

PORTER'S COLLEGE, Washington St., cor. La Salle.

HOTELS.

The Hotels of Chicago excel in the elegance, comfort, and convenience of their interior arrangements and accommodations. To the leading ones of the city would we especially call attention.

The Sherman House,

Situated on the corner of Clark and Randolph streets, is built of Athens marble, six stories in height. The building was erected in 1860, at a cost of $428,000. It has a front on Clark Street of one hundred and eighty feet, and that on Randolph Street of two hundred feet. It is furnished throughout in the most splendid and costly style, having all the accommodations and conveniences that the most luxurious taste could desire. All the rooms, beside being well furnished, lighted, and ventilated, have means of access by a perpendicular railway, intersecting each

PORTER'S
TELEGRAPH COLLEGE,
Washington St., corner La Salle St.,
CHICAGO, ILL.

SAM'L PORTER, Pres't.   E. PAYSON PORTER, Principal.

As a means of PERMANENT SUPPORT, Telegraphing competes with any other salaried business, either for gentlemen or ladies; and in addition, it never loses its novelty. Strangers are cordially invited to visit the Institution and witness its operation.

INTERIOR OF PORTER'S TELEGRAPH COLLEGE.

J. K. TYLER,
DEALER IN
HARDWARE,
SASH, WEIGHTS,
AND
WHEELING NAILS.
AMERICAN, RUSSIAN, AND ITALIAN
HEMP SASH CORD;
Russell & Erwin's, and Davenport & Mallory's
LOCKS.
BLAKE'S JAPANNED AND SILVERED
Acorn Tip Butts, etc.

The attention of Merchants and Builders is invited to my stock of Builders' Hardware, which is made a specialty, comprising the finer class of goods not generally kept by Wholesale Houses.

41 STATE St.,
(City Hotel Buildings),
CHICAGO.

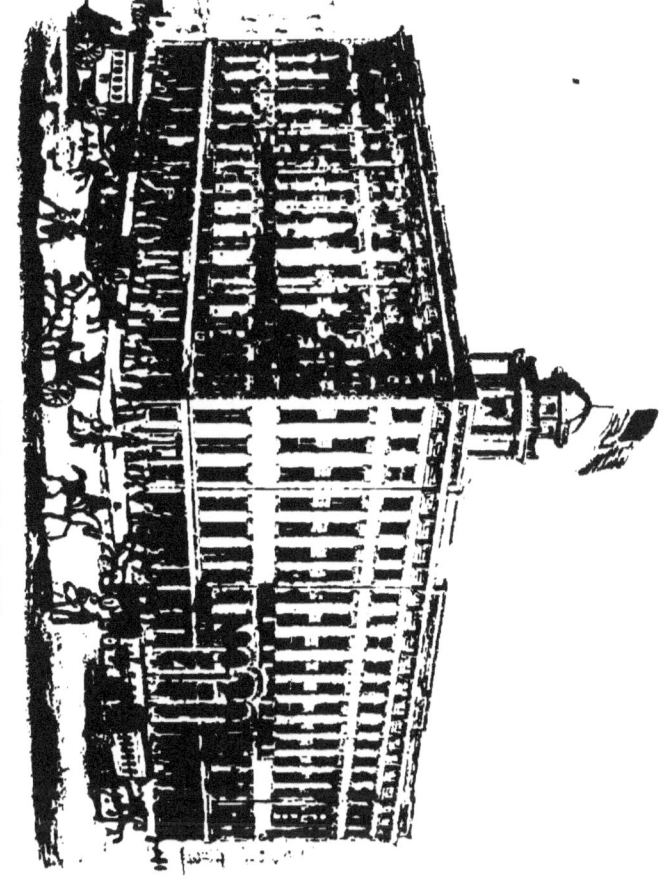

TREMONT HOUSE.
CHICAGO.

story, in addition to the broad and capacious corridors and stairways, independent of the ordinary approaches from floor to floor. Accommodations for about 700 guests. Gage & Rice, proprietors.

Tremont House.

This is another elegant establishment, located on the corner of Lake and Dearborn streets. It is constructed of brick, six stories high, and contains about three hundred rooms. It is furnished throughout with an elegance and sumptuousness unequalled by any hotel in the city, and all its internal appointments and conveniences are unsurpassed. It is well located in the very heart of the city. Messrs. Gage & Drake are its gentlemanly proprietors.

The Matteson House,

Under the management of Mr. Robert Hill, is situated corner of Dearborn and Randolph streets, convenient to the principal business routes, public buildings, railroad offices, places of amusement, &c. It is a neat and plain red brick structure, four stories high, with the modern improvements, and capable of accommodating about four hundred guests. It has been opened about sixteen years, and has well sustained its reputation as a first-class house.

St. James' Hotel.

This fine establishment, which was partially burnt in July, 1867, has been rebuilt and reopened, newly finished and fitted up in a magnificent manner, and has again taken its place among our first-class hotels. It has a capacity for about four hundred guests, with superior accommodations. Its situation, on Dearborn Street, corner of Washington, adjoining the Crosby Opera House, is in a delightful part of the city, and is a most eligible and convenient stopping-place for travellers.

The Briggs House

Is one of our most popular first-class hotels. It is five stories high, with fine accommodations for about four hundred and fifty guests. The location of this house, corner of Wells. and Randolph streets, is convenient of access to the business portion of the city, and near the Court House and Chamber of Commerce. The traveller is here provided with every possible comfort, and its table is spread with all the delicacies of the season. B. H. Skinner, proprietor.

Hall's Safe & Lock Co.

MANUFACTURERS OF

HALL'S PATENT CONCRETE FIRE AND BURGLAR-PROOF SAFES,

VAULTS, VAULT FRONTS AND
VICTOR COMBINATION BANK LOCKS.
93 Dearborn St,
CHICAGO, ILL.
and Cincinnati Ohio.

Richmond House,

Located corner of South Water Street and Michigan Avenue, has recently been renovated and refurnished throughout in splendid style, and is supplied with all the comforts and conveniences of a first-class house. The Prince of Wales selected this house as his place of sojourn during his stay in Chicago. Its location near the Great Central Depot, together with the beautiful avenue upon which it is situated, render it a most convenient and delightful stopping-place for travellers. Richard Somers, proprietor.

Adams House.

The above house, situated on the corner of Lake Street and Michigan Avenue, is another among the many popular hotels with which our city is favored. It is built of Milwaukee brick, five stories high, and cost about $250,000. It has accommodations for some three hundred guests. The house was opened in 1856. It contains all the modern improvements throughout and is one of the few hotels where it is a pleasure to stop. Pearce & Benjamin are its proprietors.

Metropolitan Hotel.

This popular house has recently been altered and greatly improved in all its internal arrangements. It has about two hundred and fifty rooms, fitted up with a view to comfort as well as elegance. The traveller who may be so fortunate as to select this house during his stay in the city will find its kind and courteous proprietor, Mr. C. W. Baldwin, ever ready and anxious to contribute to the comfort of his guests. The Metropolitan is situated on the southwest corner of Randolph and Wells streets, near the business centre of the city.

Revere House

Is situated on the north side, at the corner of North Clark and Kinzie streets. It is a first-class house, replete in all its departments with modern conveniences. Can accommodate about two hundred and fifty guests. Gilbert Dutcher, proprietor.

Barnes House.

This is an elegant hotel, located in the central part of the city, corner of Randolph and Canal streets, and convenient to the Northwestern, St. Louis, and Pittsburg, and

KLOKKE & HAND,
PRACTICAL
Hatters and Furriers,
31 NORTH CLARK STREET,
(Uhlich's Block,)
CHICAGO.

Hats, Caps, Furs, Gloves, Canes, Umbrellas, &c.
A large and Fashionable stock constantly on hand.

JOHN D. ZERNITZ,
IMPORTER OF
CHINA, GLASS,
QUEENSWARE,
LAVA, PARIAN, SILVER-PLATED WARE, TABLE CUTLERY, ETC.
No. 55 North Clark Street,
CHICAGO, ILLINOIS.

S. & P. FLORSHEIM,
DEALERS IN
Boots and Shoes,
46 NORTH CLARK STREET,
CHICAGO.
(Under the Revere House.)

A large assortment of Burt's Fine Shoes.

NEW YORK
LIFE INSURANCE COMPANY,

HOME OFFICE, 112 & 114 BROADWAY, NEW YORK.

Established 1845...................Assets, $10,000,000.

WM. H. BEERS, Actuary.   MORRIS FRANKLIN, Pres't.

North-Western Branch Office, 126 WASHINGTON ST., CHICAGO, ILL.

O. P. CURRAN, Gen. Agent.

During the twenty-three years of its existence, it has issued policies upon the lives of more than Fifty Thousand persons, and has paid to the Widows and Orphans of its members over Four Millions of Dollars, and to them (the insured) while living, over Three and One Half Millions of Dollars, as return Premiums or Dividends.

Being a purely Mutual Company, no part of its funds are diverted from its Members to pay Stockholders for use of Capital, &c. The security it offers is an amount of Assets reaching Ten Millions of Dollars. Its Trustees are men of undoubted standing, chosen from its Members, and its Funds are invested with strict regard to security. Its Annual Dividends are 50 per cent. Suicide does not cause a forfeiture of the Policy, that being considered an evidence of insanity, and insanity the result of disease.

This Company originated and introduced the New Feature known as The Non-Forfeiture Plan, which is rapidly superseding the life-long payments, and has revolutionized the system of Life Insurance in the United States, and which has since been adopted by all Life Companies; thus attesting the force of public opinion in favor of a system so favorable to policy holders as that established by the New York Life for the benefit of its Members. It has received the unqualified approval of the best business men of the land, large numbers of whom have taken out policies under it, simply as an investment.

It has also just originated a New Feature which will eclipse anything heretofore known, that will repay those contemplating insurance, for a visit to my office, directly opposite the South Door of the Court-House.

O. P. CURRAN,
General Agent.

COURT HOUSE.
(Chicago)

Fort Wayne Depots. Mr. R. B. Barnes is the worthy host of the establishment.

Garden City House.

Located corner of Madison and Market streets. This house is also situate near the Chicago and St. Louis, and Pittsburg and Fort Wayne Depots, and contains all the comforts of a first-class hotel. W. Merritt, proprietor.

NEWSPAPERS.

The oldest newspaper in Chicago is the "Evening Journal," which was founded in 1843. The "Tribune" comes second in age, but stands at the head of the city dailies, with a circulation nearly equal to the aggregate of those of the other dailies. The "Times" is the only Democratic daily issued in the city. The "Republican," first issued in 1865, is rapidly gaining its way into public favor.

We herewith append a list of all the papers and periodicals published in the city · —

Morning Dailies.

TRIBUNE, 51 South Clark Street.
TIMES, 118 Dearborn Street.

REPUBLICAN, 93 Washington Street.
STAATS-ZEITUNG, (German,) 55 La Salle Street.
UNION, (German,) 233 Randolph Street.

Evening Dailies.

JOURNAL, 46 Dearborn Street.
POST, 157 Dearborn Street.

Tri-Weeklies.

JOURNAL, 46 Dearborn Street.
REPUBLICAN, 93 Washington Street.
TIMES, 118 Dearborn Street.
TRIBUNE, 51 South Clark Street.

Sunday Papers.

TRIBUNE, 51 South Clark Street.
TIMES, 118 Dearborn Street.
REPUBLICAN, 93 Washington Street.
UNION, (German,) 233 Randolph Street.
STAATS-ZEITUNG, (German,) 55 La Salle Street.

Weeklies.

ART JOURNAL, 122 Dearborn Street.
ADVANCE, 25 Lombard's Block.
CATHOLIC WEEKLY, 47 La Salle Street.
CHRISTIAN ADVOCATE, 66 Washington Street.
CHRISTIAN FREEMAN, 110 Dearborn Street.
CHRISTIAN TIMES, 110 Dearborn Street.
JOURNAL OF COMMERCE, 71 State Street.
NEW COVENANT, 132 Clark Street.
PRESBYTERIAN, Clark and North Water Streets.

THE ADVANCE

A FIRST-CLASS

RELIGIOUS NEWSPAPER

OF NATIONAL CIRCULATION.

REV. WM. W. PATTON, D.D., EDITOR-IN-CHIEF.

Among its regular contributors are many of the best religious and literary writers in the country. It especially aims to furnish

Choice Reading For Home and Sunday,

while its Commercial Department will have

Special Value to Business Men,

as, for

Able FINANCIAL and BUSINESS EDITORIALS, Careful REVIEW of the MARKETS, Latest Corrected PRICES CURRENT,

it excels every other paper of its class in the country.

SPLENDID PREMIUMS!!

to those who get up clubs. Specimen copies always sent free.

Terms, $2.50 a year.

Address

THE ADVANCE COMPANY,
25 LOMBARD BLOCK,
CHICAGO.

POE & HITCHCOCK,
PUBLISHERS & BOOKSELLERS,
Keep the Largest Assortment of

Sunday School Books
AND
REQUISITES
IN THE WEST.
ALSO A GREAT VARIETY OF
THEOLOGICAL & MISCELLANEOUS
BOOKS, STATIONERY, ETC.

Liberal Discount given to all Ministers, and Students preparing for the Ministry, and to the Trade.

IMPORTANT TO ADVERTISERS.
P. & H. also publish the following
PAPERS,
all of which have a large circulation.

WEEKLY.
The Western Christian Advocate, at Cincinnati.
The Northwestern Christian Advocate, at Chicago.
The Central Christian Advocate, at St. Louis.
The Christian Apologist (in German), at Cincinnati.
The Sandebudet (in Swedish), at Chicago.

MONTHLY.
The Ladies' Repository — A First-Class Family Magazine, each number containing two elegant Steel Engravings.

SEMI-MONTHLY.
The Sunday School Advocate — A beautifully Illustrated Child's Paper.
The Sontag-Schul Glocke — An Illustrated Child's Paper, in German.

Address the Publishers at
S. W. cor. Main & 8th Sts., Cincinnati.
66 Washington St., Chicago.
413 Locust St., St. Louis.

PRAIRIE FARMER, 164 Clark Street.
SAVENSKA AMERIKANAREN, 157 Randolph Street.
SAENDEBUDET, 66 Washington Street.
POST, 151 Dearborn Street.
UNION, 233 Randolph Street.
REPUBLICAN, 93 Washington Street.
TRIBUNE, 57 Clark Street.
TIMES, 118 Dearborn Street.
EVENING JOURNAL, 46 Dearborn Street.
SPIRITUAL REPUBLIC, 84 Dearborn Street.
WESTERN RURAL, 84 Dearborn Street.
CHURCHMAN, 101 Washington Street.
COMMERCIAL EXCHANGE, 188 South Water Street.
MERCHANT, 140 South Water Street.
RAILROAD GAZETTE, 101 Washington Street.
TEMPERANCE ADVOCATE, 109 Monroe Street.
PRICE CURRENT, 164 Clark Street.
WORKINGMEN'S ANTI-MONOPOLY, 155 Clark Street.
IRISH REPUBLIC, Randolph and Dearborn Streets.
NEW REPUBLIC, 170 Clark Street.
TEMPLARS' OFFERING, 168 Clark Street.
GERMAN REFORM, 101 Washington Street.
STAATS-ZEITUNG, 55 La Salle Street.
RELIGIO-PHILOSOPHICAL JOURNAL, 88 Dearborn St.

Semi-Monthlies.

HOME VISITOR, 110 Dearborn Street.
RELIGIONS-HAUSFREUND, (German,) 38 La Salle St.

Monthlies.

AMERICAN PULPIT, 148 Lake Street.
WESTERN PULPIT, 110 Dearborn Street.

OLIVE WREATH, Reynolds' Block.
HOME PAPERS, 147 Clark Street.
HOME VISITOR, 110 Dearborn Street.
LITTLE BOUQUET, 88 Dearborn Street.
THE GREAT WEST, Reynolds Block.
LITTLE CORPORAL, 138 Lake Street.
JOLLY JOKER, Opera House.
MEDICAL JOURNAL, 91 Dearborn Street.
MEDICAL EXAMINER, State and Monroe Streets.
INVESTIGATOR, 147 Clark Street.
LADIES' REPOSITORY, 66 Washington Street.
MANFORD'S MAGAZINE, Madison and Dearborn St.
MYSTIC STAR, 110 Dearborn Street.
SUNDAY SCHOOL TEACHER, 155 Randolph Street.
RATTA HEMLANDET, 192 Superior.
MEDICAL AND SURGICAL JOURNAL, 147 Clark Street.
VOICE OF MASONRY, 164 Clark Street.
MISSIONARY ADVOCATE, 66 Washington Street.

Quarterlies.

AMERICAN LAW MANUAL, 80 La Salle Street.
MEDICAL AND SURGICAL JOURNAL, 147 Clark St.

CHURCHES.

There are about one hundred and forty churches in the city of Chicago, very many of which are distinguished for their elegance and architectural beauty. They are always to be found open on the Sabbath-day, and strangers are invited to attend. They will find a welcome to the House of the Lord, and a seat at the table of the Master with their brethren. Services commence at 10½ o'clock A. M.; 3½ and 7½ P. M. We annex a full list of all the churches in the city.

Baptist.

First	Wabash Av. & Hubbard.
Second	Monroe and Morgan Sts.
Wabash Avenue	Wabash Av. cor. 18th St.
Union Park	Wabash Av. c. Paulina.
Fifth	Harrison & Sangamon Sts.
North	Superior cor. N. Dearborn
Indiana Avenue	Indiana Av. cor. 30th St.
First German	Indiana Av. cor. Wood St.
First Danish	Indiana Av. cor. Union St.
Second German	Curtis cor. Third St.
First Swedish	Reuben Street
Olivet, (colored,)	Fourth Avenue n. Polk St.
Free Will	Peoria cor. Jackson St.

Congregational.

Plymouth	Wabash Av. c. Eldridge Ct.
Union Park	Reuben c. W. Washington.
New England	N. Dearborn c. S. White.
Tabernacle	c. Morgan & W. Indiana.
First	Green c. W. Washington.
South	26th St. and Calumet Av.
Salem	Oakland Av. cor. Lake St.

Church of God.

First	Warren cor. Robey Street.

Christian.

First.........................Cass near Michigan Av.
Second......................Centralia and Front Sts.

Episcopal.

Cathedral....................W. Washington c. Peoria.
St. James'...................Cass and Huron Sts.........
St. John's...................Lake St. c. St. John's Pl.
St. Mark's...................Cottage Grove Avenue.
St. Stephen's................Forquer n. Blue Is'nd Av.
St. Luke's...................Wabash Av. cor. 16th St.
St. Ansgarius................Indiana cor. Franklin St.
Trinity......................Wabash Av. and Jackson.
Grace........................Wabash Av. and Peck Ct.
Holy Communion...............Wabash Av. & Randolph.
Ascension....................La Salle and Maple Sts.
Christ.......................Michigan Av. & 24th St.
Atonement....................Madison and Robey Sts.

Friends.

First Society................Room 15, Methodist Block.

German Evangelical.

Erste Evangelische...........Polk cor. Third Avenue.
Zweite.......................Chicago Av. cor. Wells St.
Evangelic Association........Twelfth cor. Union Sts.

Hebrew.

Sinai........................Van Buren cor. Third St.
Kehilath.....................Wells and Adams Sts.
Kehilo Benay Shalem..........Harrison and Fourth Av.
Zion.........................Desplaines n. Madison St.

Independent.

First........................,........Illinois, near Wells St.

Lutheran.

First Norwegian............N. Franklin and Erie Sts.
Second Norwegian..........W. Indiana & Peoria Sts.
Swedish ....Superior, near Wells St.
Vor Fraelsers................Third, cor. May St.
Salem.........................21st, near Archer Ave.
Zion...........................Union, cor. Mitchel St.
Emanuel......................Brown and W. Taylor Sts.
Trinity........................Harrison, cor. Kossuth St.
St. John's....................Chicago Av. cor. Noble St.
St. Paul's....................Ohio, cor. N. La Salle St.
St. Paulus'...................Superior, cor. Franklin St.

Methodist.

First..........................Clark and Washington Sts.
First Scandinavian.........Illinois, n. Nth. Market St.
Second Scandinavian......Fourth & Sangamon Sts.
Maxwell......................Newbury & Maxwell Sts.
Wesley........................Sedgwick & Black Hawk.
Park Avenue.................cor. Robey and Park Ave.
Bridgeport....................Bonfield Street.
Trinity........................Indiana Av. and 21st St.
Centenary....................Monroe, n. Morgan Sts.
Grace..........................La Salle, cor. Chicago Av.
Wabash Avenue............Wabash, cor. Harrison St.
West Indiana................Indiana and Sangamon.

Methodist, (German.)

Van Buren	Van Buren, n. Clark St.
Maxwell	Maxwell, n. Johnson St.
Clybourne	Clybourne Av., Division.

Methodist, (African.)

Quinn's Chapel	Jackson, cor. Fourth Av.
Bethel Chapel	Griswold, n. Harrison St.

Presbyterian, (New School.)

First	Wabash Av. n. Congress.
Second	" cor. Washington.
Third	Washington & Carpenter.
Seventh	cor. Halsted and Harrison.
Eighth	Washington, cor. Robey.
Ninth	Ellis Av. nr. Wahpanseh.
Westminster	Dearborn, cor. Ontario.
Calvary	Indiana Ave., cor. 22d St.
Olivet	Wabash Av., cor. 14th St.
Hyde Park	Hyde Park.

Presbyterian, (Old School.)

First Scotch	226 Clark Street.
North	Indiana Ave., cor. Cass.
South	Wabash Ave. & Congress.
Central	Cass, near Illinois Street.
Jefferson Park	Jackson, cor. Peoria.
Reformed	Fulton, near Clinton.
Fullerton Avenue	Fullerton Av., near Clark.

Presbyterian, (United.)

First	W. Green, near Madison.
Third	Superior & N. Franklin.

ROOT & CADY

67, WASHINGTON STREET. — **OPERA House BLOCK, CHICAGO**

Wholesale AGENTS in the Northwest for the celebrated MASON & HAMLIN CABINET ORGAN

ALL KINDS OF GENERAL MUSICAL MERCHANDISE

MUSIC PUBLISHERS, Importers AND Wholesale Dealers in BAND AND ORCHESTRAL INSTRUMENTS, STRINGS

Full Catalogue embracing all branches of our business furnished on application.

G. F. ROOT   E. T. ROOT   C. M. CADY

Reformed Dutch.

First..................Foster, near Polk.
Second................Monroe & Sangamon.

Roman Catholic.

Cathedral..................State, cor. Superior.
Notre Dame................Tyler and Halsted Sts.
Holy Family...............West 12th, cor. May St.
Immaculate Conception...N. Franklin, nr. Schiller.
St. Mary's................Wabash Ave. & Madison.
St. Patrick's.............Desplains, cor. Adams.
St. Louis'................Sherman, near Polk.
St. Columbia's............Paulina, cor. Indiana St.
St. John's................Clark, cor. 18th St.
St. James'................Prairie Ave., cor. 27th St.
St. Boniface's............cor. Cornell and Noble.
St. Bridget's.............Bridgeport.
St. Joseph's..............Chicago Ave., cor. Cass.
St. Michael's.............cor. North Av. & Church.
St. Francis'..............Clinton and Mather.
St. Wenceslaus'...........Desplains and Dekoven.

Spiritualists.

First Society.............Crosby Music Hall.
Independent...............Washington Hall.

Swedenborgians.

New Jerusalem.............Adams, nr. Michigan Av.
German....................Reuben, nr. Chicago Ave.
Mission...................cor. 33d & Kankakee Av.

Unitarians.

Messiah...................Wabash Av. & Hubbard Ct.
Unity.....................Chicago Av. & Dearborn.

Universalists.

Redeemer......................Wash'gton & Sangamon.
St. Paul's....................Wabash Av. & Van Buren.

United Brethren in Christ.

First........................Clinton, cor. Wilson St.

CEMETERIES.

Graceland....................Green Bay Road.
German Catholic..............Green Bay Road.
Anshe Mayrew.................Green Bay Road.
Old City.....................Green Bay Road.
Rose Hill....................Green Bay Road.
Oakwood......................Cottage Grove.

STEAMBOATS.

For Buffalo and Cleveland, foot of N. Dearborn St.
For Two Rivers, from Rush Street Bridge.
For Lake Superior, from Rush Street Bridge.
For Sarnia and Lake Superior, from foot of La Salle.
For Milwaukee and Green Bay, fr. Rush St. Bridge.
For Grand Haven and Muskegon, fr. Rush St. Bridge.

RAILROADS.

It was in April, 1849, that the whistle of the locomotive was first heard on the prairies

THE NEW COVENANT;
A WEEKLY UNIVERSALIST PAPER,
CHICAGO, Ill.

EDITED BY D. P. & M. A. LIVERMORE.

This is one of the largest and best Universalist papers in the denomination. Price $2.50 per year. Address

Rev. D. P. LIVERMORE,
Chicago, Ill.

Universalist Books.

A large assortment of Universalist and Sunday School Books, constantly on hand at the New Covenant Office.

PROOF TEXTS
OF
ENDLESS PUNISHMENT
EXPLAINED.

384 Pages.

BY REV. D. P. LIVERMORE.

This Book contains a careful examination of all the Texts quoted to prove the Doctrine of Endless Punishment; such as:—"The wicked shall be turned into hell;" "In hell he lifted up his eyes, being in torment;" "These shall go away into everlasting punishment;" "Our God is a consuming fire," etc. Price $1.25. Postage 20 cts. Address

Rev. D. P. LIVERMORE,
"New Covenant," Chicago, Ill.

FAVORITE ROUTE EAST.

MICHIGAN SOUTHERN RAILROAD LINE.

Four Express Trains leave daily from New Depot, corner Van Buren and Sherman Sts., Chicago, for all points East. Drawing-Room Compartment Cars on Morning Express Trains through to

CLEVELAND

WITHOUT CHANGE.

Luxurious and most comfortable

SLEEPING CARS

on Night Trains. Only two Changes between

CHICAGO AND NEW YORK.

☞ This is the only line running the Drawing-Room Cars out of Chicago.

For Tickets and all information, apply at General Office, **56 Clark St.** (under Sherman House), or at the **Depot**.

SAMUEL C. HOUGH,
General Passenger Agent.

MICHIGAN SOUTHERN & ROCK ISLAND RAILROAD DEPOT.
Chicago

west of Chicago. The railroad system, of which this city is now the centre, embraces over five thousand miles of track. A passenger train reaches or leaves the city every fifteen minutes of the twenty-four hours. Not less than two hundred trains arrive or depart in a day and night. There are sixteen points on the Mississippi River which have railroad communication with Chicago. It is but fifteen years since this city first had railroad connection with the cities on the Atlantic coast; and the traveller now has his choice of three main lines, which branch out to every important intermediate point.

The depots are immense in extent, and admirably convenient. There are two for passengers only,—the Central, foot of Lake Street, and the Michigan Southern, on Van Buren Street, each of which have under cover three-quarters of a mile of track, from which three trains can start at the same moment without the least danger of interference, and wherein no person has to cross a track in changing cars.

The following are the locations of the depots of the various lines diverging from Chicago, together with a list of the towns and distances on the several routes

A GUIDE TO CHICAGO.

For arrival and departure of trains the daily papers must be consulted; the changes with the seasons being so frequent as to preclude the possibility of affixing a permanent table here.

Omnibuses run to and from the hotels and depots on the arrival and departure of all trains. Fare fifty cents.

Michigan Southern and Northern Indiana Railway.

This road runs from Chicago to Toledo, Ohio, and Detroit, Michigan. It makes connections at White Pigeon with the branch to Three Rivers; at Adrian, with the branch for Jackson; and also with branch for Monroe and Detroit.

The entire length of the road, with branches, is about 550 miles. Depot, corner of Sherman and Van Buren streets. State-Street cars run the nearest to the depot of any line.

Distances and Stations from Chicago to Toledo (via Adrian).

STATIONS.	MILES.	STATIONS.	MILES.
Chicago to		Holmesville	50
Chicago Junction	6	Laporte	59
Ainsworth	12	Rolling Prairie	66
Pine Station	22	Carlisle	72
Miller's	30	Terre Coupee	74
Calumet	41	South Bend	86
N. A. and S. Crossing	49	Mishawaka	90

A GUIDE TO CHICAGO.

STATIONS.	MILES.	STATIONS.	MILES.
Elkhart	101	Osseo	183
Bristol	109	Pittsford	187
Middlebury	114	Hudson	193
White Pigeon	120	Clayton	200
Sturgis	131	Adrian	211
Burr Oak	138	Palmyra	216
Bronson	144	Blissfield	220
Coldwater	155	Knight's	222
Quincy	161	Sylvania	232
Allen's	168	Air Line Junction	241
Jonesville	173	Toledo	244
Hillsdale	178		

Distances and Stations from Chicago to Toledo (via Air Line).

STATIONS.	MILES.	STATIONS.	MILES.
Chicago to		Wawaka	130
Chicago Junction	6	Brimfield	136
Ainsworth	11	Kendalville	143
Pine Station	22	Corunna	149
Miller's	29	Lawrence	151
Calumet	41	Waterloo	155
N. A. and S. Crossing	49	Jarvis	163
Homesville	50	Edgerton	170
Laporte	58	Bryan	180
Rolling Prairie	65	Styker	186
Carlisle	72	Archibald	192
Terre Coupee	73	Pettisville	197
South Bend	85	Wasseon	202
Mishawaka	89	Delta	210
Elkhart	101	Centerville	214
Goshen	111	Springfield	224
Millersburg	119	Air Line Junction	241
Sigonier	126	Toledo	244

Pittsburg, Fort Wayne, and Chicago Railway.

This may be termed an "air line" route, as it is the most direct one to Pittsburg, Philadelphia, and New York. It is composed of several roads, which were consolidated in

1858. The entire distance from Chicago to Pittsburg is 468 miles.

The following are the connections made with other roads. At Wanatah, with the Louisville and New Albany Road; at Plymouth, with the Cincinnati, Peru, and Chicago Road; at Fort Wayne, with Toledo and Wabash; at Lima, with the Dayton and Michigan; at Forest, with Sandusky, Dayton, and Cincinnati Road; at Crestline, with the Cleveland and Columbus Road; at Mansfield, with Sandusky, Mansfield, and Newark Road; at Orville, with the Cleveland, Zanesville, and Cincinnati Road; at Alliance, with Cleveland and Pittsburg Road; at Homewood, with New Castle and Beaver Valley Road; and at Pittsburg, with the Pennsylvania Central and boats on the Ohio River.

Depot corner Madison and Canal streets, which may be reached by Madison-Street line of cars.

Stations and Distances from Chicago to Pittsburg.

STATIONS.	MILES.	STATIONS.	MILES.
Chicago to		Hanna	59
Rock Island Junction	7	Grovertown	74
Ainsworth	12	Plymouth	84
Clarke	24	Inwood	90
Hobart	33	Bourbon	94
Wheeler	37	Warsaw	108
Valparaiso	44	Pierceton	117
Wanatah	53	Huntsville	121
Morgan	56	Columbia	129

STATIONS.	MILES.	STATIONS.	MLS.
Arcola	139	Shreve	323
Fort Wayne	148	Wooster	333
Naples	158	Orville	344
Dixon	167	Lawrence	351
Van Wert	180	Massillon	358
Middlepoint	187	Canton	366
Delphos	193	Louisville	373
Lima	207	Strasburg	378
Lafayette	215	Alliance	384
Johnstown	222	Damascus	392
Washington	229	Salem	398
Dunkirk	231	Franklin	401
Forest	238	Columbiana	408
Upper Sandusky	250	Palestine	418
Nevada	258	Enon	422
Bucyrus	267	New Galilee	427
Robinson	273	Homewood	433
Crestline	279	New Brighton	439
Richland	284	Rochester	442
Mansfield	292	Leetsdale	453
Lucas	299	Sewickley	455
Perrysville	307	Haysville	457
Loudonville	311	Allegheny	467
Lakeville	317	Pittsburg	468

Chicago and Great Eastern Railway.

This road runs from Chicago to Cincinnati, a distance of 294 miles, and connects Chicago with the South and Southwestern States. It makes connections at Kokomo with the Peru and Indianapolis Road, forming a direct route to Louisville, Nashville, and Lexington, Ky.; at Anderson, with the Bellefontaine Railway; at Logansport, with the Toledo, Logansport, and Burlington Road, and Toledo, Wabash, and Western; at Richmond, with the Xenia,

Dayton, and Western Road, and the Columbus and Indianapolis Road.

The depot of this road is corner of Canal and Kinzie streets, on the north side.

Distances and Stations from Chicago to Cincinnati.

STATIONS.	MILES.	STATIONS.	MILES.
Chicago to		Florida	171
N. W. Junction	4	Anderson	177
C. B. and Q. Crossing	5	Middletown	184
St. Louis Crossing	7	Honey Creek	187
R. I. Crossing	15	Sulphur Springs	190
Ill. Cent. Crossing	20	New Castle	197
Dolton	21	Ashland	200
Lansing	27	Millville	203
Joliet Crossing	32	Hagarstown	208
Crown Point	41	Washington	215
Hebron	51	Centerville Pike	218
Kouts	61	Richmond	224
N. A. and S. Crossing	68	Florence	234
North Judson	77	Eaton	241
Shakapee	81	Barnet's	248
Winamac	92	Camden	250
Star City	98	Somerville	255
Rosedale	101	Collinsville	258
Royal Centre	106	Seven Mile	262
Gebhard	112	Hamilton	269
Logansport	117	Schenck's	272
Anoka	122	Jones	275
Walton	126	Elliston	277
Lincoln	130	Glendale	279
Galveston	133	Lockland	282
Kokomo	139	Carthage	284
Tampico	145	Spring Grove	287
Nevada	149	Ludlow	289
Windfall	152	Brighton	292
Curtisville	158	O. and M. Junction	293
Quincy	161	Cincinnati	294
Frankton	166		

Chicago, Alton, and St. Louis Railway.

Trains for St. Louis and intermediate stations leave the depot corner of Madison and Canal streets. Passengers may take the Madison-Street line of cars for the depot.

This road forms an air line route to St. Louis, making connections as follows:—At Joliet, with Rock Island Road; at Chenoa, with Toledo, Peoria, and Warsaw Road; at Normal, with Illinois Central; at Bloomington, with St. Louis and Jacksonville Road; at Springfield, with Toledo, Wabash, and Western Railway; at Monticello, with St. Louis and Jacksonville Road; at Alton, with Terre Haute and Alton Road; and at St. Louis, with the Pacific and North Missouri Railways, and Mississippi steamers for points West and South.

Distances and Stations from Chicago to St. Louis.

STATIONS.	MILES.	STATIONS.	MILES.
Chicago to		Dwight	74
Fort Wayne Junction	2	Odell	82
Bridgeport	4	Cayuga	87
Summit	12	Pontiac	92
Wells Springs	18	Ocoya	98
Lemont	26	Chenoa	103
Lockport	33	Lexington	111
Joliet	38	Towanda	119
Elwood	46	Normal	124
Hampton	49	Bloomington	126
Wilmington	53	Shirley	133
Stewart's Grove	58	Funk's Grove	137
Gardner	65	McLean	141

STATIONS.	MILES.	STATIONS.	MILES.
Atlanta	146	Nilwood	214
Lawn Dale	150	Carlinville	223
Lincoln	157	Macoupin	230
Broadwell	164	Plainview	234
Elkhart	168	Shipman	238
Williamsville	174	Miles	243
Sherman	178	Brighton	245
Springfield	185	Monticello	252
T. W. and W. Junction	187	Alton	257
Wood Side	191	Milton	261
Chatham	194	Mitchell	269
Auburn	200	Kinder	274
Virden	206	Venice	276
Girard	210	St. Louis	280

Illinois Central Railroad.

This road, extending from Chicago to Cairo, a distance of 365 miles, was completed in 1856.

In its passage through the State it makes the following connections:—At Matteson, with Joliet and Northern Indiana Road; at Gilman, with Toledo, Peoria, and Warsaw, and Toledo, Logansport, and Burlington Roads; at Tolono, with Toledo, Wabash, and Western Road; at Mattoon, with Terre Haute, Alton, and St. Louis Road; at Odin, with the Ohio and Mississippi Road; at Centralia, with the Dunleith branch of the Illinois Central; and at Cairo, with the Mobile and Ohio Road; also with boats on the Ohio and Mississippi Rivers. Depot, foot of Lake Street.

WHOLESALE
BOOTS, AND
22 LAKE ST.

WHITNEY BOOT
MANUFACTURED BY

DEALERS IN
SHOES.
CHICAGO.

WHITNEY Bro's & YUNDT.

Distances and Stations from Chicago to Cairo.

STATIONS.	MILES.	STATIONS.	MILES.
Chicago to		Neoga	185
Calumet	14	Effingham	199
Thornton	24	Watson	206
Matteson	28	Mason	212
Richton	29	Edgewood	215
Monee	34	Farina	223
Peotone	40	Kinmundary	229
Manteno	47	Tonti	239
Kankakee	56	Odin	244
Chebanse	64	Centralia	253
Clifton	69	Richview	263
Ashkum	73	Ashley	266
Gilman	81	Coloma	274
Onarga	85	Tamoroa	280
Spring Creek	88	Du Quoin	289
Loda	99	De Soto	302
Paxton	103	Carbondale	308
Pera	109	Makanda	317
Rantoul	114	Cobden	323
Champaign	128	Jonesboro	329
Tolono	137	Wetang	341
Pesotum	142	Ullin	345
Tuscola	150	Pulaski	349
Okaw	158	Villa Ridge	353
Milton	164	Mounds	357
Mattoon	173	Cairo	365

Michigan Central Railroad.

This is the direct route to Canada via Detroit. The road was completed in 1852.

It makes connections at Michigan City with the Louisville, New Albany, and Chicago Railway; at Jackson, with the Amboy, and Lansing Road; also with the Jackson Branch of the Michigan Southern to Adrian; and at Detroit, with the Grand Trunk and Great Western Roads of Canada.

A GUIDE TO CHICAGO.

Cars leave the Great Central Depot, foot of Lake Street.

Distances and Stations from Chicago to Detroit.

STATIONS.	MILES.	STATIONS.	MILES.
Chicago to		Kalamazoo	141
Stock Yards	5	Galesburg	150
Calumet	15	Battle Creek	164
Gibson's	24	Marshall	177
Lake Station	36	Albion	188
Porter	44	Parma	198
Michigan City	56	Jackson	208
New Buffalo	66	Grass Lake	219
Avery's	75	Chelsea	230
Dayton	83	Dexter	237
Buchanan	87	Ann Arbor	247
Niles	93	Ypsilanti	255
Dowagaic	106	Wayne	267
Decatur	117	Dearborn	274
Lawton	125	Grand Trunk Junction	281
Mattawan	129	Detroit	284
Ostemo	135		

Chicago, Burlington, and Quincy Railroad.

This road leads from Chicago to Galesburg, from which place it extends to two different points on the Mississippi River—one to Quincy, Illinois, and the other to Burlington, Iowa.

In its route it forms connections with the Illinois Central Road at Mendota; Galesburg, Peoria, and Lewiston Road, at Galesburg; Burlington and Missouri River Road, at Burlington; Quincy and Toledo Road, at Camp Point; Quincy and Palmyra Road, at Quincy. At the latter place it connects with the Hannibal and St. Joseph Road. The cars leave from the Central Depot, foot of Lake Street.

Distances and Stations from Chicago to Quincy.

STATIONS.	MILES.	STATIONS.	MILES
Chicago to		St. Augustine	181
Lyons	13	Avon	185
Downer's Grove	23	Prairie City	188
Napierville	30	Bushnell	194
Aurora	40	Bardolph	198
West Aurora	41	Macomb	206
Oswego	45	Colchester	212
Bristol	48	Tennessee	214
Plano	54	Colmar	220
Sandwich	58	Plymouth	224
Somanauk	62	Augusta	228
Leland	68	La Prairie	235
Earle	75	Keokuk Junction	238
Mendota	85	Camp Point	243
Arlington	94	Coatsburg	248
Malden	101	Paloma	251
Princeton	107	Fowler	254
Wyanet	113	Cliola	256
Buda	119	Quincy	265
Neponsit	125		
Kewanee	133		
Galva	142		
Altona	149		
Oneida	153		
Wataga	157		
Galesburg	165		
Abingdon	175		

The Road from Galesburg to Burlington — 45 miles — passes through the towns of Cameron, Monmouth, Young America, and Oquawka Junction.

Chicago and Rock Island Railroad.

This line is composed of the Chicago and Rock Island, Peoria and Bureau Valley, and Mississippi and Missouri Railroads. It leads from Chicago to Council Bluffs and Omaha

City on the Missouri River. It is finished thus far to Kellogg, 315 miles from Chicago.

At Bureau it connects with the Valley Road to Peoria, 47 miles; at Wilton, with the branch to Muscatine and Washington.

The depot is located corner of Sherman and Van Buren streets.

Distances and Stations from Chicago to Kellogg.

STATIONS.	MILES.	STATIONS.	MILES.
Chicago to Junction	7	Atkinson	152
Blue Island	16	Genesee	159
Bremen	23	Colona	170
Mokena	30	Moline	179
Joliet	40	Rock Island	182
Minooka	51	Davenport	184
Morris	62	Walcott	196
Seneca	72	Fulton	201
Marseilles	77	Durant	203
Ottawa	84	Wilton	209
Utica	94	Moscow	212
Lasalle	99	Atalissa	217
Peru	100	West Liberty	222
Trenton	110	Iowa City	238
Bureau	114	Oxford	253
Tiskilwa	122	Marengo	269
Pond Creek	129	Victor	281
Sheffield	137	Brooklyn	289
Annawan	146	Grinnell	304
		Kellogg	315

Chicago and North-Western Railway.

This road embraces the original North-western line which runs from Chicago to Fort Howard and Green Bay, Wisconsin, and also the Galena and Chicago Union, with its many branches. Since the consolidation it is one of the most important roads running from Chicago. Depot, corner of Canal and Kinzie streets.

Wisconsin Division.

Making connections at Harvard Junction, with the Branch to Rockford, also to Beloit and Madison; at Clinton Junction, with the Western Union Road; at Watertown with the Milwaukee and St. Paul Road; at Burnett, with the Horicon Road; at Oshkosh, with the steamers on Lake Winnebago and Wolf and Fox rivers; and at Fort Howard, with steamers on Green Bay to Escanaba, and there connecting with the Peninsular Road for Marquette on Lake Superior.

Distances and Stations from Chicago to Green Bay.

STATIONS.	MILES.	STATIONS.	MILES.
Chicago to		Watertown	130
Des Plaines	17	Juneau	145
Dunton	22	Minnesota Junction	148
Palatine	26	Burnett	152
Barrington	32	Chester	160
Crystal Lake	43	Oakfield	168
Woodstock	51	Fon Du Lac	177
Harvard Junction	63	Oshkosh	194
Lawrence	65	Neenah	207
Clinton Junction	78	Appleton	214
Janesville	91	Wrightstown	226
Milton Junction	99	De Pere	236
Fort Atkinson	111	Fort Howard	242
Jefferson	117	Green Bay	244

Chicago and Northwestern Railway.
(Galena Division.)

Making connections at the Junction with the Chicago, Burlington, and Quincy Road; at Elgin, with the Fox River Valley Road; at Belvidere, with the Madison Branch; and at Freeport, with the Illinois Central for Dunleith and Dubuque on the Mississippi River. Depot, corner of North Wells and North Water streets.

Stations and Distances from Chicago to Freeport.

STATIONS.	MILES.	STATIONS.	MILES.
Chicago to		Huntley	55
Harlem	9	Union	62
Cottage Hill	16	Marengo	66
Babcock's Grove	20	Garden Prairie	72
Danby	23	Belvidere	78
Wheaton	25	Cherry Valley	84
Winfield	28	Rockford	92
Junction	30	Winnebago	99
Wayne	35	Pecatonica	106
Clintonville	39	Ridott	114
Elgin	42	Freeport	121
Gilbert's	50		

Chicago and Northwestern Railway.
(Madison (Wis.) Division.)

Making connections at Harvard with the Rockford Division. Depot, corner North Water and North Wells streets.

FIELD, LEITER & CO.,

DRY GOODS,

110 112, 114, 116

LAKE STREET,

Chicago.

ALLEN & MACKEY,

CARPETINGS,

BRYAN HALL, 89 SOUTH CLARK STREET,
CHICAGO.

OIL-CLOTH, MATTINGS,

PAPER-HANGINGS

CURTAIN MATERIALS AND TRIMMINGS,

UPHOLSTERY AND FURNISHING GOODS,

BEDDING AND FEATHERS,

THE LARGEST STOCK IN CHICAGO,

WHOLESALE AND RETAIL,

At prices that will compete successfully for any trade against the Eastern Markets.

MAYNARD BROTHERS,
FIRE AND BURGLAR-PROOF
Safes, Vault Doors, &c.

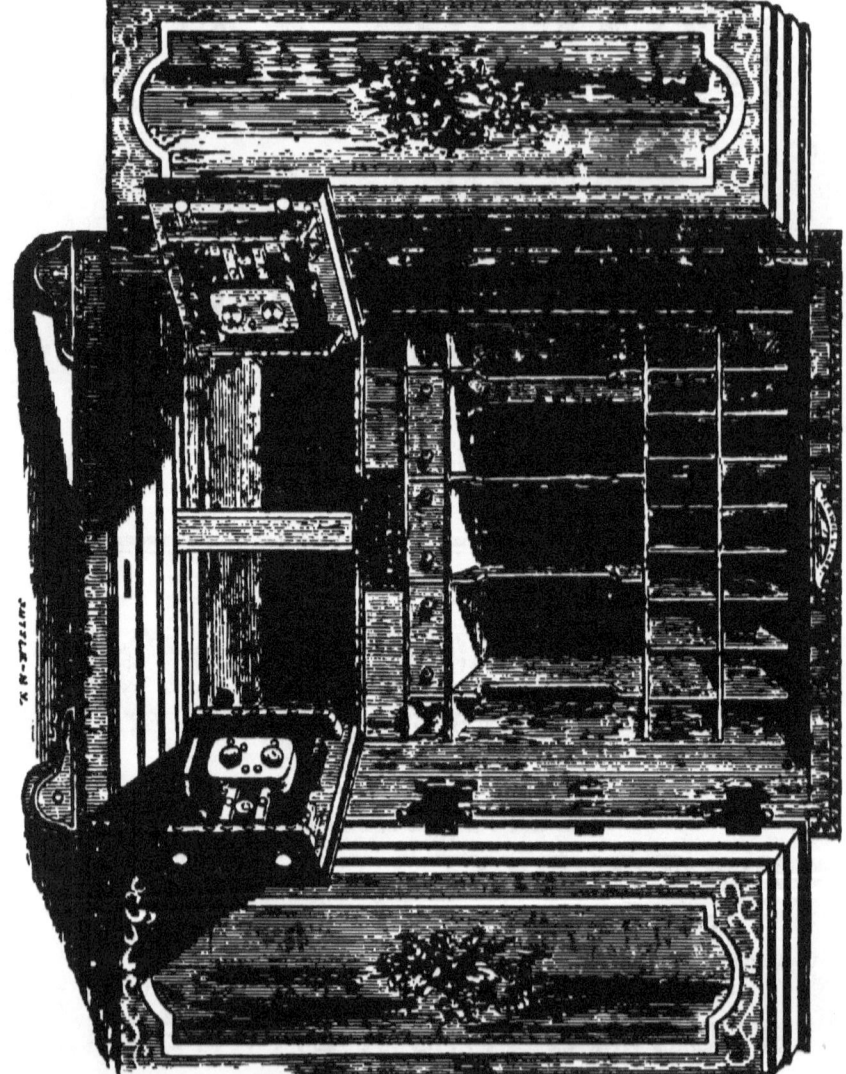

Yale's Bank and Small Locks,
84 WASHINGTON STREET, CHICAGO.
Call and see the Latest Improvements.

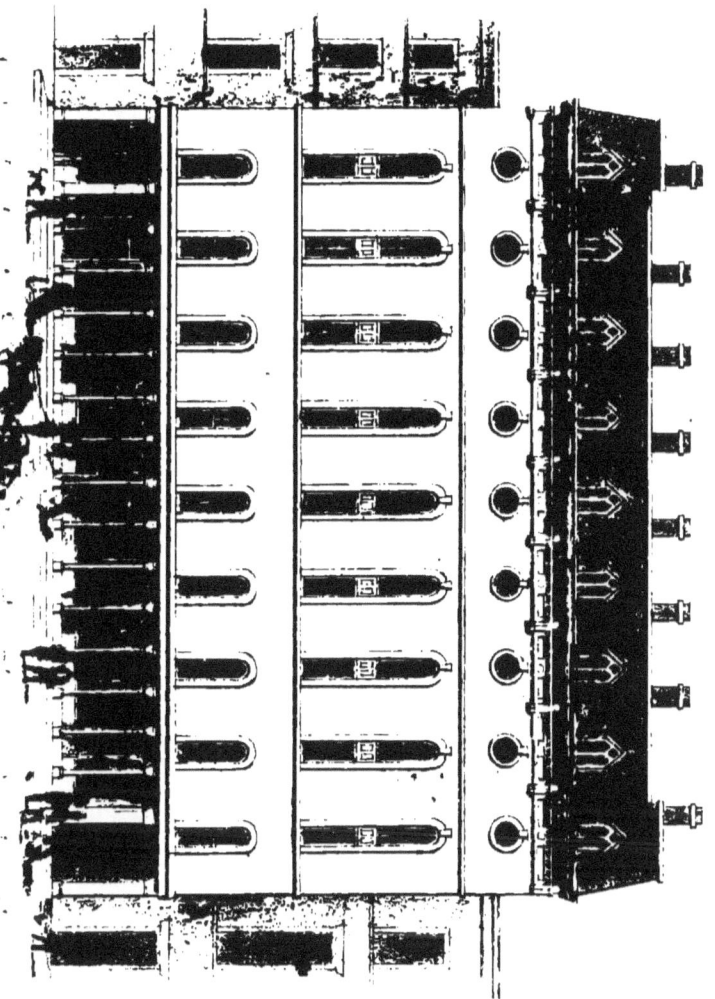

YOUNG MEN'S CHRISTIAN ASSOCIATION BUILDING.
Chicago
Destroyed by Fire Jan'y 7th 1868.

A GUIDE TO CHICAGO.

Stations and Distances from Chicago to Madison.

STATIONS.	MILES.	STATIONS.	MILES.
Chicago to		Roscoe	84
Des Plaines	17	Beloit	90
Dunton	22	Afton	98
Palatine	26	Hanover	103
Barrington	32	Footville	106
Crystal Lake	43	Magnolia	110
Woodstock	51	Evansville	115
Harvard	63	Oregon	127
Caledonia	78	Madison	138

Chicago and Northwestern Railway.

(Fox River Valley Division.)

Making connections at Elgin with the Galena Division; at Crystal Lake, with the Wisconsin Division; and at Genoa, with the Rockford Branch.

Stations and Distances from Chicago to Genoa Lake.

STATIONS.	MILES.	STATIONS.	MILES.
Chicago to		Algonquin	52
Harlem	9	Crystal Lake	56
Cottage Hill	16	C. and N. W. Crossing	57
Babcock's Grove	20	Nunda	60
Danby	23	McHenry	65
Wheaton	25	Ringwood	69
Winfield	28	Richmond	75
Junction	30	Genoa	77
Elgin	42	Geneva Lake	85
Dundee	47		

Chicago and Northwestern Railway.

(Iowa Division.)

Making connections at the Junction with the Galena Division, and Fox River Valley Line; at Dixon, with the Illinois Central; at Ful-

171

ton, with steamers on the Mississippi River Depot, corner of North Wells and North Water streets.

Stations and Distances from Chicago to Omaha.

STATIONS.	MILES.	STATIONS.	MILES.
Chicago to		Lowdon	178
Harlem	9	Mechanicsville	195
Cottage Hill	16	Mount Vernon	203
Babcock's Grove	20	Cedar Rapids	219
Danby	23	Blairstown	244
Wheaton	25	Tama	270
Winfield	28	Marshal	289
Galena Junction	30	State Centre	303
Geneva	36	Nevada	318
La Fox	41	Boonsboro	340
Blackberry	44	Moingona	346
Lodi	50	Des Moines	349
Cortland	55	Ogden	352
De Kalb	58	Beaver	357
Malta	64	Hager	364
Dement	70	New Jefferson	370
Rochelle	75	Scranton	379
Ashton	83	Glidden	389
Franklin	88	Carroll	396
Nachusa	93	Tip Top	406
Dixon	98	Vail	415
Nelson	104	Denison	424
Sterling	110	Elkton	432
Galt	113	Dunlap	441
Round Grove	119	Woodbine	451
Morrison	124	St. John's	461
Fulton	136	Honey Creek	476
Clinton	138	Crescent	481
Low Moor	148	Council Bluffs	490
Dewit	157	Omaha	493

Chicago and Milwaukee Railway.

This road was opened in 1855. It now belongs to the consolidated line of the Chicago and Northwestern Railroad. The distance from Chicago to Milwaukee is 85 miles.

At Kenosha it connects with the Rockford Division; at Racine, with the Western Union Road.

Depot, corner of Canal and Kinzie streets.

Stations and Distances from Chicago to Milwaukee.

STATIONS.	MILES.	STATIONS.	MILES.
Chicago to		Waukegan............	35
Rosehill.................	8	State Line............	45
Evanston..............	12	Kenosha...............	52
Winnetka..............	16	Racine Junction.....	60
Glencoe................	19	Racine.................	62
Highland Park.......	23	County Line..........	71
Lake Forest..........	28	Oak Creek............	76
Rockland..............	30	Milwaukee............	85

CITY RAILWAYS.

The "Chicago City Railway Company" run their cars in the "South Division," upon the following routes:—

State Street Line.

Starting from the corner of State and Lake streets; run up State Street to Thirty-First Street. Return same route.

Cottage Grove Line.

From State and Lake streets, up State Street to Twenty-Second Street, out Twenty-Second to Cottage Grove Avenue, and thence to Douglas Place, where are the Soldiers'

Home and the Douglas Monument. The Chicago University is in the immediate vicinity. Cars return same route.

Indiana Avenue Line.

From State and Lake up State to Twenty-Second, out Twenty-Second to Indiana Avenue, and thence to Thirty-First Street, where is the Race-Course. The cars return by Indiana Avenue to Eighteenth Street, and thence out to State Street, and down State to Lake. This route passes the Orphan Asylum, Old Ladies' Home, and Erring Woman's Refuge.

Archer Avenue Line.

From State and Lake streets, up State to Nineteenth Street and Archer Avenue; up Archer Avenue to Halsted Street. Return same way. This route terminates at Bridgeport and in the immediate vicinity of the Great Stock Yards.

The "West Division Railway Company" run their cars upon the following streets:—

Randolph Street Line.

From State and Randolph streets, running west on Randolph Street to Bryan Place, and

Manufacturers of and Dealers in

TWINES AND CORDAGE,

Cotton & Flax Duck All Widths and Weights

COTTON AND FLAX TWINES,

Of Every Description

TENTS & AWNINGS, TARPAULINS, WAGONS & HORSE COVERS

Of Plain or Rubber Coated Duck Constantly on hand or made to Order,

205 & 207 S^T WATER S^T

Corner of Wells, **CHICAGO.**

G. Hubbard.   J. S. Turner.   Geo. P. Carpenter

thence out Lake Street to Western Avenue or city limits. Return same route. This is the nearest line to the Artesian Wells.

Madison Street Line.

Starting from State and Lake streets, up State to Madison, and thence to Western Avenue. Return same route.

Milwaukee Avenue Line.

From Randolph and State streets, out Randolph to Halsted, through Halsted to Milwaukee Avenue, and thence to Western Avenue. Return the same way.

Blue Island Avenue Line.

Starting from Randolph and State streets, through Randolph, Halsted, and Blue Island Avenue, to Twenty-second Street. Some of the cars of this line run out Madison Street, and thence out Blue Island Avenue.

Clinton Street Line.

From Randolph and State streets, through Randolph and Clinton, to Meagher Street. Return same route.

The different routes of the "**North Division Railway**" are as follows:—

North Clark Street Line.

Starting from State and Lake streets, pass across the river, up North State Street, to Michigan Street; through Michigan Street to North Clark, and thence to Fullerton Avenue or city limits. These cars pass the City Cemetery and Lincoln Park. Passengers can take the dummy cars at city limits for Lake View or Graceland Cemetery.

Chicago Avenue Line.

From State and Lake streets, out North State Street to Chicago Avenue, and thence to north branch of Chicago River. Return the same way.

Sedgwick Street Line.

From State and Lake streets, through North State, North Clark, Division and Sedgwick streets, to North Avenue.

Clybourne Avenue Line.

From North Clark Street Bridge, through Clark, Division, and Clybourne Avenue, to Fullerton Avenue or city limits.

Larabee Street Line.

From North Clark Street Bridge, through Clark, Chicago Avenue, and Larabee Street, to city limits.

Fare, six cents on any of the city railroads. Ten fares, indicated on one card, are sold for fifty cents.

HACKS AND CARRIAGES.

For the benefit of strangers and others, we give the rates of fare in the city of Chicago, to be taken by or paid to the owner or driver of any licensed hack or carriage. We trust it will serve as a safeguard to strangers against the impositions frequently practised upon them by the drivers of these conveyances.

The Hack-Stands are on the streets around the Court House.

For conveying a passenger, not exceeding one mile, **50 cts.**

For every additional passenger of the same party, . **25 cts.**

For conveying a passenger any distance over a mile, and not more than two miles, ... **$1.00**

For each additional passenger of the same party, . **25 cts.**

For carrying a passenger any distance exceeding two miles, ... **$1.50**

For each additional passenger of the same party, when the distance is over two miles, ... 50 cts.

For conveying children between five and fourteen years of age, half of the above prices may be charged for like distances; but for children under five years of age, no charges shall be made: *Provided*, that the distance from any railway depot, steamboat landing, or hotel, to any other steamboat landing, railroad depot, or hotel, shall in all cases be estimated as not exceeding one mile.

For the use, by the day, of any hackney-coach or other vehicle drawn by two horses or other animals, with one or more passengers, ... $6.00

For the use of any such carriage or vehicle by the hour, with one or more passengers, with the privilege of going from place to place, and stopping as often as may be required, as follows: For the first hour, $1.50; for the second hour, 75 cents; for each succeeding hour, 50 cents.

Every passenger shall be allowed to have conveyed upon such vehicle, without charge, his ordinary travelling baggage; not exceeding, in any case, one trunk and twenty-five pounds of other baggage. . For every additional package, where the whole weight or baggage is over one hundred pounds, if conveyed to any place within the city limits, the owner or driver may collect 15 cents.

THE CHICAGO TIMES
GREATLY ENLARGED AND IMPROVED.

The Leading Democratic, News and Commercial Paper of the Northwest.

THE CHICAGO TIMES has lately been greatly improved, having adopted the QUARTO FORM, and enlarged its dimensions equal to twenty-five per cent, of its former size. It is now

THE LARGEST PAPER PRINTED IN CHICAGO, and no pains or expense are spared to make it the BEST.

The several editions of THE TIMES consist as follows:

THE DAILY EDITION. — Issued every morning except Sunday.

THE TRI-WEEKLY EDITION. — Issued on Tuesday, Thursday, and Saturday mornings.

THE WEEKLY EDITION. — Issued on Tuesday.

THE SUNDAY TIMES. — Issued on Sunday Morning.

THE DAILY EDITION.
One Year..$12.00
Six Months...................................... 6.00
Three Months................................... 3.00

THE TRI-WEEKLY EDITION.
One Year..$6.00
Six Months...................................... 3.00
Three Months................................... 1.50

THE WEEKLY EDITION.
Single Copy, One Year......................$2.00
Single Copy, Six Months................... 1.00
Club of Five Copies, One Year............ 9.00
Club of Ten Copies, One Year.............17.50
Club of Twenty Copies, One Year.........33.00

THE SUNDAY EDITION.
One Year..$2.50
Six Months...................................... 1.25
Sent with the other Editions at the rate, per year, of.................................... 2.00

All orders should be addressed to the Publishers. Specimen numbers will be sent free on application.

W. F. STOREY & CO.

THE
ATLANTIC MUTUAL
Life Insurance Co.
OF
ALBANY, NEW YORK,

Issues Policies on all the popular plans of Insurance, and offers the following SPECIAL ADVANTAGES: —

Ten Per Cent. Deduction from usual rates to Practical Homœopathists.

ANNUAL DIVISION OF PROFITS.

IMMEDIATE PAYMENT OF LOSSES.

All Policies incontestable and non-forfeitable.

Liberal Provisions to Travellers,

And by SPECIAL ACT,

The State of New York guarantees the value of its Policies.

Officers:

ROBT. H. PRUYN, President. | JAMES HENDRICK, Vice-Pres't.
LOUIS B. SMITH, Secretary.

G. D. BEEBE,
Gen'l Western Agent.
66 Clark Street. (under Sherman House,)
Chicago, Ill.

RAILROAD DISTANCES.

For the convenience of travellers, we append a table of distances from Chicago to the principal cities in the United States.

CHICAGO TO	MILES.	CHICAGO TO	MILES.
Albany, N. Y.	810	Memphis, Tenn.	679
Augusta, Ga.	1,602	Montreal, Canada	824
Atlanta, Ga.	1,814	New Haven, Ct.	1054
Baltimore, Md.	826	New York	899
Boston, Mass.	1,010	New Orleans, La.	2,518
Buffalo, N. Y.	539	Pittsburg, Pa.	468
Burlington, Vt.	915	Portland, Me.	1,130
Cleveland, Ohio	356	Providence, R. I.	960
Columbus, Ohio	271	Petersburg, Va.	1,040
Concord, N. H.	930	Philadelphia, Pa.	823
Cincinnati, Ohio	294	Quebec, Canada	1,002
Canandaigua, N. Y.	629	Reading, Pa.	771
Charleston, S. C.	1,430	Richmond, Va.	1,144
Detroit, Mich.	284	Rochester, N. Y.	599
Elmira, N. Y.	675	Savannah, Ga.	1,579
Harrisburg, Pa.	717	Springfield, Mass.	906
Hartford, Ct.	948	St. Paul, Minn.	389
Indianapolis, Ind.	210	St. Louis, Mo.	280
Louisville, Ky.	321	Toledo, Ohio	240
Lynchburg, Va.	1,240	Wilmington, Del.	820
Milwaukee, Wis.	85	Wilmington, N. C.	1,310
Macon, Ga.	1,810	Washington, D. C.	998
Mobile, Ala.	2,400	Worcester, Mass.	966

WATERING-PLACES, &c.

For reference by the tourist and pleasure-seeker, we give a list of the more prominent Watering-Places, Springs, and fashionable resorts.

CHICAGO TO   MILES.

Avon Springs, N. Y.	1,070
Atlantic City, N. J.	904
Bedford Springs, Pa.	760
Brandywine Springs, Del.	956
Blue Lick Springs, Ky.	374
Cape May, N. J.	890
Cape Ann, Mass.	1,040
Carlisle Springs, Pa.	738
Catskill Mountains, N. Y.	960
Columbia Springs, N. Y.	907
Clarendon Springs, N. Y.	940
Delaware Water Gap, Pa.	806
Drennon Springs, Ky.	340
Falls of Montmorenci, Canada	1,012
" " St. Anthony, Minn.	406
Greenwood Lake, N. Y.	868
Harrodsburg Springs, Ky.	383
Lebanon Springs, N. Y.	870

A GUIDE TO CHICAGO.

CHICAGO TO

	MILES.
Lake George, N. Y.	840
" Champlain, N. Y.	876
" Mahopac, N. Y.	900
" Memphremagog, Vt.	1,114
Long Branch, N. J.	900
Lake Winnipiseogee, N. H.	1,033
Mount Vernon, Va.	1,019
Mount Holyoke, Mass.	970
Mammoth Cave, Ky.	406
Nahant, Mass.	1,022
Niagara Falls, N. Y.	579
Newport, R. I.	1,030
Natural Bridge, Va.	1,188
Richfield Springs, N. Y.	715
Rockaway Beach, L. I.	920
Saratoga Springs, N. Y.	831
Sharon Springs, N. Y.	740
Shannondale Springs, Va.	1,040
Schooley's Mountains, N. J.	842
Trenton Falls, N. J.	739
White Mountains, N. H.	1,106
West Point, N. Y.	887
Weir's Cave, Va.	1,121
Willoughby Lake, Vt.	1,098
Warm Springs, N. C.	1,436
White Sulphur Springs, Va.	1,104
Yellow Springs, Pa.	860

TO TRAVELLERS.

1. Purchase your ticket previous to entering the cars, thus saving yourself trouble and a *dime*.

2. Check your baggage, thereby avoiding any anxiety or vexation.

3. Have regard for the rights of your fellow-travellers, thereby teaching them by example to respect yours.

4. The fact of any article being deposited in a seat is evidence of the seat having been taken.

5. Always show your ticket (without getting in a bad humor) whenever the conductor asks for it. Observe this rule, and it will pay.

6. Look out for your valise, carpet-bags, &c., (as professional thieves are always around,) especially when the cars stop at a dining station.

7. A gentleman or lady should not occupy more than one seat at a time.

8. *Ladies* without escort in travelling should be very particular with whom they become acquainted.

The business of this Company is confined EXCLUSIVELY to the Insurance of First-Class, Healthy Lives.

SPECIAL FEATURES.

THE STOCK PLAN
By which the full cash effect of the premium is rendered

IMMEDIATE, SECURE, AND CERTAIN
In lieu of a dividend, which is Distant, Contingent, and Uncertain.

LOSSES PAID IN THIRTY DAYS
After due notice and proof of Death.

UNIVERSAL LIFE INSURANCE COMPANY.
A GOOD MAN Leaveth an INHERITANCE. PROV. XIII. 22.
1855

OF NEW YORK.

REVERSIONARY DIVIDENDS
100 Per Cent!
OR
CASH DIVIDENDS IN ADVANCE,

No Notes taken on which the Insured must pay interest, or to be deducted from the amount of the Policy at death.

All Policies have a CASH Surrender Value.

Office Western Department, - - - 21 La Salle Street, Chicago.
CHARLES GILMAN SMITH, M.D. *Medical Director.*
T. ORMSBEE, *Manager.*

☞ *RELIABLE AGENTS AND SOLICITORS WANTED. APPLY TO THE MANAGER.* ☜

SHOENFELD BROTHERS,

DRY GOODS

AND
NOTIONS,

35 & 37 N. Clark Street, corner of Kinzie,

(Uhlich's Block,)

CHICAGO.

SAMUEL J. CAVEN. LOUIS H. PERLEY.

CAVEN & PERLEY,
GENERAL
Commission Merchants,
FOR THE SALE AND PURCHASE OF
Grain, Poultry, Butter, Game, Dressed Hogs, Eggs, Furs, Green and Dried Fruits,

160 SOUTH WATER STREET,
CHICAGO, ILL.

MACKENZIE'S
10,000 RECEIPTS.

"The most extensive and reliable work of the kind ever printed." — *Michigan Reporter*, 8mo. 11, '67.

MACKENZIE'S 10,000 RECEIPTS,
A UNIVERSAL ENCYCLOPÆDIA.

"The most important Family book ever issued."— *Rural American, N.Y.*, 8mo. 4, 1866.

BUY IT.

T. ELLWOOD ZELL,
Publisher, Philada.

9. "If your lips would save from slips,
   Five things observe with care:
   Of whom you speak,—to whom you speak,—
   And how,—and when,—and where."

10. Whenever you see a fellow over-anxious for your comfort, and pushing himself forward, saying, "Are you travelling alone?"—"Allow me to," &c., &c.,—just say to him, "Thank you, sir. I require no assistance." By observing this rule, ladies will often save themselves and others trouble.

11. Never sit in a seat, in warm weather, with a man weighing 244 pounds.

12. Never give information without being asked, then you will not be contradicted.

13. Never let your valise, bag, coat, or any other article, occupy a seat when there is a rack for them. It looks bad for you to occupy a whole seat when there are passengers standing without seats.

14. Never sit on the end of another person's seat with your back turned, talking to an opposite party;—it is disagreeable to the one whose seat you are thus obtruding yourself on.

15. Never sit beside a person who is hard of hearing, and has never travelled any; get away; there are too many questions to be answered.

16. Never make love in a railroad car; being too affectionate, people will talk.

17. All railroad tickets are GOOD UNTIL USED; the condition "good for this day only" being of no value, according to judicial decisions.

EMPIRE SPRING BED CO.,
No. 90 MONROE STREET, CHICAGO.

The best SPRING BED in the WORLD. Costs only $7.

Fits any kind of Bedstead. Packs in small compass for shipment.

Full directions sent with goods for putting up the bed. Any one can do it. AGENTS WANTED. **S. F. BOUTON**, *Gen. Western Agent*

SCHOOL PUBLICATIONS OF
ELDREDGE & BROTHER,
17 & 19 SOUTH SIXTH ST., PHILADELPHIA.

A NEW EDITION OF THE CLASSICS.

The attention of teachers is directed to

CHASE & STUART'S CLASSICAL SERIES.

Edited by THOMAS CHASE, A.M., Prof. of Classical Literature, Haverford College; GEORGE STUART, A.M., Prof. of the Latin Language, Central High School, Philadelphia.

THE SERIES, WHEN COMPLETE, WILL CONSIST OF

CÆSAR'S COMMENTARIES, CICERO'S ORATIONS, VIRGIL'S ÆNEID, HORACE AND SALLUST.

The Publishers claim particular merit for this edition of the Classics, and beg leave to note the following important particulars: Purity of Text; Judicious Arrangement of the Notes; Beauty of Mechanical Execution; the Low Price at which the Volumes are sold.

CÆSAR'S COMMENTARIES

ON THE GALLIC WAR, with Explanatory Notes, Lexicon, and Geographical Index, by GEORGE STUART, A.M., Professor of the Latin Language, Central High School, Philada. 16mo. 264 pages. Price $1.25.

The references in this volume are made partially to HARKNESS'S LATIN GRAMMAR, and ANDREWS & STODDARD'S LATIN GRAMMAR. In accordance with the suggestions of many prominent educators, the references will in future editions be made to both of these Grammars.

VIRGIL'S ÆNEID, with explanatory notes, by Thomas Chase, A.M.

ELASTIC SPONGE.

MATTRESSES,

PILLOWS, CHURCH, CAR

AND OTHER CUSHIONS.

Full size Mattress, ... $30.00

Pillows, per pair, ... 5.50

Far Superior every way to best Curled Hair.

Call or send for FREE pamphlet, and direct your orders to

WESTERN ELASTIC SPONGE CO.

192 & 194 Lake St., Chicago.

ST. LOUIS BRANCH, 720 Fifth St.

DETROIT BRANCH, 78 Griswold St.

Where we also manufacture.

ORPHAN ASYLUM
Chicago.

GIRARD
Fire Insurance Co.

NEW OFFICE,
639 N. E. cor. Chestnut & Seventh Streets,
PHILADELPHIA.

Capital and surplus, · · · $350,000.

All of which is safely invested in Real Estate, Bonds, and Mortgages, Government Loans, and other good Securities.

This Company have successfully insured

$100,000,000

Of property in the last fourteen years, and paid more than 800 losses by fire.

It has nearly doubled its capital in this period. It has never belonged to any combination of underwriters in this city, or out of it.

Our Agents in Pennsylvania, and elsewhere, *have not been instructed* to join any organization for establishing arbitrary rates and rules.

DIRECTORS.

THOMAS CRAVEN,	ALFRED S. GILLETT,
FURMAN SHEPPARD,	N. S. LAWRENCE,
THOMAS MACKELLAR,	CHARLES I. DUPONT,
JOHN SUPPLEE,	HENRY F. KENNEY,
JOHN W. CLAGHORN,	JOSEPH KLAPP, M D.

SILAS YERKES, Jr.

THOMAS CRAVEN, *President*
ALFRED S. GILLETT, *Vice-Pres't & Treas.*
JAMES B. ALVORD, *Secretary.*

Mackenzie's 10,000 Receipts,
Mackenzie's 10,000 Receipts,
Mackenzie's 10,000 Receipts.

Mackenzie's Universal Encyclopædia,
Mackenzie's Universal Encyclopædia,
Mackenzie's Universal Encyclopædia.

BY A LARGE CORPS OF EXPERTS.

Containing valuable and practicable information on almost every conceivable subject.

Notice a few Recommendations.

"A book of great value."—Gov. A. G. CURTIN.

"I regard Mackenzie's Book as the most valuable secular book ever issued."—Dr. WM. HAUSER, Jefferson Co., Ga.

"Contains an *immense* number of practical recipes and a great deal of other information respecting the Useful and Domestic Arts, Agriculture, Medicine, Manufactures, Dyeing, &c., not forgetting Rinderpest and Trichinæ."—NEW YORK TRIBUNE.

Foundry Established 1823.

J. FAGAN & SON

STEREOTYPE
FOUNDERS

Are prepared to execute by the Plaster, Cla[y] and Copper modes of Stereotyping, orders f[or] every description of Plain and Ornament[al] Book and Music Work, in every variety a[nd] style of type. Also, Plate Alterations an[d] Repairs, Map-Lettering, Engraving Plate[s,] Blocking on Metal or Wood, and

ALL KINDS OF STEREOTYPE WORK.

Estimates of the probable cost of Stereotyping furnished on a[p]plication.

621 & 623 Commerce Street,

PHILADELPHIA.

Caxton Press.

Sherman & Co.'s

BOOK MAKING

AND

JOB PRINTING

ESTABLISHMENT.

CAXTON PRESS TRADE MARK.

Stereotyping and Electrotyping; Ruling and Binding; Engraving and Lithographing; and every description of Printing neatly executed, with practical and personal supervision. Book and Job PAPERS and CARDS made to order. STATIONERY supplied at market rates.

☞ *Fire-proof Vaults for Storage of Stereotype Plates.*

Cor. Seventh & Cherry Sts.
𝔓𝔥𝔦𝔩𝔞𝔡𝔢𝔩𝔭𝔥𝔦𝔞.

STREET, MOORE & CO.,
PUBLISHERS,
Booksellers & Stationers.

BIBLES AND PRAYER-BOOKS
AT WHOLESALE.

EPISCOPAL CHURCH BOOK DEPOSITORY

CHURCH FURNITURE, DECORATIONS,

STAINED GLASS WINDOWS,

CLERICAL VESTMENTS, &C.

DESIGNING AND ILLUMINATING.

101 Washington St., near Clark,

CHICAGO.

C. A. STREET.   R. E. MOORE.   J. P. KELLY.

www.ingramcontent.com/pod-product-compliance
Lightning Source LLC
Chambersburg PA
CBHW020805230426
43666CB00007B/858